GREAT MYSTERIES

Reincarnation

OPPOSING VIEWPOINTS®

Look for these and other exciting *Great Mysteries: Opposing Viewpoints* books:

GREAT MYSTERIES

Reincarnation

OPPOSING VIEWPOINTS®

by Michael Arvey

Greenhaven Press, Inc.   P.O. Box 289009, San Diego, California 92128-9009

No part of this book may be reproduced or used in any other form or by any other means, electrical, mechanical, or otherwise, including, but not limited to, photocopy, recording, or any information storage and retrieval system, without prior written permission from the publisher.

Library of Congress Cataloging-in-Publication Data

Arvey, Michael.
　　Reincarnation : opposing viewpoints / by Michael Arvey.
　　　　p.　cm. — (Great mysteries)
　　Includes bibliographical references.
　　Summary: Explores the mysteries of reincarnation, a centuries-old theory of what happens to us after we die. Examines the possible proof and several alleged case histories of reincarnation.
　　ISBN 0-89908-067-7
　　1. Reincarnation—Juvenile literature. [1. Reincarnation.] I. Title. II. Series: Great mysteries (Saint Paul, Minn.)
BL515.A78　1989
133.9′01′3—dc20　　　　　　　　　　　　　89-37443
　　　　　　　　　　　　　　　　　　　　　　　CIP
　　　　　　　　　　　　　　　　　　　　　　　AC

"We are each of us passengers in the exploration of a vast universe within ourselves, a dynamic, ever-restless kaleidoscope of images, ideas, dreams, emotions, and more, the complexity and extent of which we have scarcely as yet begun to grasp."

— *Ian Wilson*

Contents

Introduction

This book is written for the curious—those who want to explore the mysteries that are everywhere. To be human is to be constantly surrounded by wonderment. How do birds fly? Are ghosts real? Can animals and people communicate? Was King Arthur a real person or a myth? Why did Amelia Earhart disappear? Did history really happen the way we think it did? Where did the world come from? Where is it going?

Great Mysteries: Opposing Viewpoints books are intended to offer the reader an opportunity to explore some of the many mysteries that both trouble and intrigue us. For the span of each book, we want the reader to feel that he or she is a scientist investigating the extinction of the dinosaurs, an archaeologist searching for clues to the origin of the great Egyptian pyramids, a psychic detective testing the existence of ESP.

One thing all mysteries have in common is that there is no ready answer. Often there are *many* answers but none on which even the majority of authorities agrees. *Great Mysteries: Opposing Viewpoints* books introduce the intriguing views of the experts, allowing the reader to participate in their explorations, their theories, and their disagreements as they try to explain the mysteries of our world.

But most readers won't want to stop here. These *Great Mysteries: Opposing Viewpoints* aim to stimulate the reader's curiosity. Although truth is often impossible to discover, the search is fascinating. It is up to the reader to examine the evidence, to decide whether the answer is there—or to explore further.

"Penetrating so many secrets, we cease to believe in the unknowable. But there it sits nevertheless, calmly licking its chops."
H.L. Mencken, American essayist

Prologue

The Question of Reincarnation

Some believe that when a person dies, his or her soul goes to an eternal place such as heaven. Others believe the soul reincarnates, enters another body to experience a new life.

One of humanity's oldest questions and greatest mysteries is what happens to us after we die. One answer, but just as great a mystery, is reincarnation. This is the theory that when we die, our souls are reborn into new bodies. For example, a person who is an American student now may have been a member of a Viking tribe or a Russian baker in a past life. A person who is male now might have been female before.

Joe Fisher, in his book *The Case for Reincarnation*, writes that throughout history people have believed in reincarnation. Ancient myth and fable, tribal memory, archaeological discoveries, and belief among followers of the world's great religions and cultures all offer proof of this. They "all testify to ages long forgotten when reincarnation, much more than . . . it is today, was a commonly accepted law of life."

Belief in reincarnation persists. In 1969, the Gallup organization did an opinion poll on the question of reincarnation. It surveyed Protestants and Catholics in twelve western countries, including the U.S. Reincarnation is not a traditional belief of these religions, yet surprising percentages of believers showed up: in

MORTAL AND IMMORTAL BODIES.

W.M.Craig, del.

Austria, 20 percent; Canada, 26 percent; France, 23 percent; Great Britain, 18 percent; Greece, 22 percent; the Netherlands, 10 percent; Norway, 14 percent; Sweden, 12 percent; United States, 20 percent; and in West Germany, 25 percent. In 1980, another Gallup poll was taken, this time aimed at the general population in the U.S. The poll indicated that 23 percent believed in reincarnation.

Why Reincarnation?

Why are people attracted to this belief? One reason is that reincarnation, if it is true, contains within it some of life's richest secrets: Where do we go when we die? Have we lived before? How is reincarnation or rebirth possible? Is choice involved? What happens between lives?

Another reason is that, to many people, reincarnation offers consolation from fear of death. After all, there is nothing to fear if life goes on.

Death comes to all people. But is death the end?

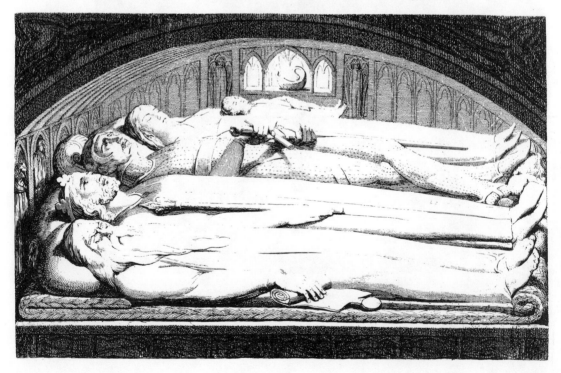

To others, reincarnation offers opportunity to strive for perfection. Each life can be used to improve oneself. For example, in one life a person could work on becoming more self-confident; in another, becoming more compassionate toward humanity and all forms of life.

In some cultures the belief in reincarnation has been so strong people have felt compelled to take their own lives. Honorable forms of suicide have long been a part of the Japanese military culture, for example. By dying honorably, the Japanese warrior felt assured of being reborn into a new, noble life. During the last days of World War II, when Japan was losing the war to America, Japanese fighter pilots, called kamikazes, would purposely slam their planes into American warships. Moreover, throughout the war in the Pacific, fearless Japanese ground soldiers avoided surrender and capture by making suicidal attacks. They would rush headlong into fierce machine gun fire—certain death. These Japanese soldiers believed that by dying for their country, they would be reborn seven times to again serve their country. This kind of suicide was considered a noble way of dying. It was the warrior's way.

This is an extreme example of the impact of reincarnation on its believers. Most religions that espouse reincarnation do not believe taking one's own life is right.

Why Not Reincarnation?

Many people reject the idea of reincarnation. Some are unhappy enough with their present life that they do not want to return. Swiss psychiatrist Carl Jung (1875-1961) comments in his book, *Memories, Dreams, Reflections*: "There are also quite a few who have been so buffeted by life, or who feel such disgust for their own existence, that they far prefer absolute cessation [end] to continuance."

Other people reject the idea of another life for

''Everything reincarnates— from subatomic particles to the swirling universe.''

Author Joe Fisher

''What the myths or stories about a life after death really mean, or what kind of reality lies behind them, we certainly do not know.''

Carl Jung, Swiss psychiatrist

This drawing, based on an old Japanese print, shows the custom of harakiri, a suicide ritual considered honorable in old Japan.

philosophical reasons. For example, the scientific world bears a materialistic viewpoint of life: Life consists of matter and energy. There is no god or individual soul. Author Sylvia Cranston, in her article "Reincarnation: Lost Chord of Christianity?" writes that atheists and other nonbelievers see reincarnation as wishful thinking. However, Cranston adds, reincarnation's rejection "could spring from a similar thinking: *one does not want it to be true.*"

Reincarnation contradicts some people's religious beliefs. Sylvia Cranston and Carey Williams, coauthors of the book *Reincarnation, A New Horizon in Science, Religion, and Society*, write, "Consider the fundamentalists and born-again Christians. They prefer an everlasting stay in heaven to the painstaking work of returning to earth to struggle more diligently for their redemption. The usual Christian notion is that when one dies, he or she faces Judgment Day, and goes to heaven or hell."

Genius Reborn?

Regardless of whether we believe in reincarnation, it might be a fact yet unproven. Consider an astonishing story Joe Fisher cites in *The Case for Reincarnation*. He writes that in August 1971, Frank De Felitta and his wife, Dorothy, were outside their home in Los Angeles "when they suddenly heard brilliant ragtime piano playing coming from the house. Rushing inside, they were amazed to find their six-year-old son, Raymond, dexterously running his hands up and down their piano keyboard which he had never before attempted to play." Raymond exclaimed his fingers were moving by themselves!

His parents, however, did not think the mystery was so wonderful. They could not understand what was happening.

According to Fisher, the boy's father later said that Raymond's behavior "was not consistent with anything we had been given to understand. It was

Some children seem to be born with exceptional talents. Are these prodigies reincarnations of persons who have developed their gifts throughout their lives?

beyond my comprehension. From never even experimenting with the piano as some young children do, here was my tiny son playing like a professional for up to five hours a day."

Raymond De Felitta grew up to be an accomplished and recognized jazz player. What could explain such behavior? How could a six-year-old suddenly play like a pro?

The famous classical composer of the eighteenth century, Wolfgang Amadeus Mozart, also was a musician of unbelievable talent when he was only a child. He wrote a piano concerto and a sonata when he was five years old! Another often-cited instance of early childhood genius is the seventeenth-century mathematician Blaise Pascal. He developed a geometric system before he was eleven years old. Did De Felitta, Mozart, and Pascal develop amazing skills in past lives that surfaced again in their new ones?

Such are some examples of the reincarnation mystery. In the next chapter, we will see more.

One

Reincarnation in Perspective

Benjamin Franklin, at the age of twenty-two, did a strange thing—he wrote his epitaph. In it, he compared himself as an old man to a tattered book. Franklin believed he would "Appear Once More In a New and more Elegant Edition Revised and Corrected by the Author."

Franklin's epitaph contains a distinct reincarnationist flavor. A practical person, he thought he would be recycled after his death. In *The Works of Benjamin Franklin*, he wrote: "When I see nothing annihilated and not a drop of water wasted, I cannot suspect the annihilation of souls, or believe that [God] will suffer the daily waste of millions of minds ready made that now exist, and put himself to the continual trouble of making new ones. Thus, finding myself to exist in the world, I believe I shall, in some shape or other, always exist."

Why have people throughout history, like Franklin, believed in reincarnation?

Renewal

Although the reincarnation concept has become popular in western countries only in recent years, the

Opposite: Benjamin Franklin, a wise and inventive man who believed life did not simply end at death.

The old life dies and the new is born. Drawing by Nelly Pogany in *The Song Celestial*, a 1934 translation of the Indian holy book *Bhagavad-Gita*.

idea has stuck like honey to the human mind since primitive times.

The basic idea remains the same: We, or some part of us, are reborn. As Voltaire, the eighteenth-century French philosopher and author said, "It is not more surprising to be born twice than once; everything in nature is resurrection."

What does Voltaire mean by resurrection? Since the beginning of humanity, people have observed the cyclical nature of life. Seasons come and go. In the fall, nature readies itself for a long sleep through winter. Trees shed their leaves. Animals hibernate. Insects lay their eggs and die. In the spring, nature again awakens. Life is renewed.

For ages, humans have witnessed this process. In *The Case for Reincarnation*, Joe Fisher writes, "For our ancestors, going to the grave was to return to Mother Earth with her boundless capacity for rebirth. To die was to be reborn."

He suggests how the idea of reincarnation may have come into being. "As civilization slowly evolved from a scattered tribal lifestyle, primal instincts of renewal, which had inspired sacred myth and lent meaning to the rigors of day-to-day survival, became the doctrine of reincarnation." In other words, the instinct for survival led to the belief in survival even after death.

Fisher remarks that even the universe displays cosmic cycles. In physics, scientists have a model for the creation and destruction of the universe, called the "big bang" theory. Some physicists believe that billions of years ago, the universe exploded outward from its core, like a firecracker. Sometime in the future, it eventually will stretch to its limits, and like a balloon, explode, only inward. It will, it is believed, collapse to its original state, and then start all over again. Fisher quotes astrophysicist John Gribbin as saying the universe "rolls on forever in an eternal cycle

"Reincarnation appears fantastic today to most adherents of the Judaeo-Christian religion; but this is only because it diverges from the ideas of life and death to which they have been habituated from childhood. For when these are viewed objectively, they are seen to be more paradoxical than that of reincarnation."

Philosopher C.J. Ducasse

"There is scarcely a religion that does not accept the continuance of life beyond death in one form or another."

Author and lecturer Hans Holzer, *Life After Death*

The big bang theory supposes that the universe, as we know it, was created by a tremendous explosion. The planets and stars were formed by the fragments flying outwards.

in which death is merely a necessary prelude to rebirth.''

Primitive Beliefs

According to Fisher, tribal communities as widespread as North and South America, Australia, Asia, Africa, and Indonesia have believed in reincarnation. Among some North American Indian tribes it was a custom ''to give a pregnant woman charms made of the hair of the dead relative whose rebirth was wished for,'' writes Fisher.

Among Eskimos, when an elderly man knew he was nearing death, he would approach a young couple and ask to be reborn into the couple's family.

David Christie-Murray, in *Reincarnation, Ancient Beliefs and Modern Evidence*, says that in Africa, ''the Bassongo [people] think that when the body disintegrates at death, the soul goes first to God in the center of the earth; after between two months and two years it becomes homesick, asks to return to earth, and resurrects in a child about to be born. Some common scar or mark proves that the baby is the deceased [dead person] reborn.''

Furthermore, he writes that in northern Nigeria it is believed souls of the dead hover in tree branches near their old homes. The souls wait for a chance to enter the wombs of women.

Some tribes viewed reincarnation as a way to improve their lot. Christie-Murray notes an interesting anecdote from Australia where it apparently was common for underprivileged black natives to wish to be reborn as white people. Sir George Grey, a white man, was the governor of South Australia in the nineteenth century. He was once identified by an old Australian woman as her reincarnated son. Her son was a black convict going to his execution and exclaimed on the way to his death, ''Me jump up Whitefellow!'' The man believed he would ''jump up'' in his next life to be a member of the privileged white race!

In some countries, Fisher says, the deaths of children were thought to be filled with meaning about life and death. For example, the African Ibo tribe believed stillborn babies resulted from souls deciding not to be reborn into another life of suffering. In some

In Nigeria, some people believe that the souls of the dead hover in trees waiting to be reborn into new babies.

Pythagoras, the ancient mathematician.

other countries, parents would bury a dead child under the front of their homes. They hoped this would draw the child back to be reborn in the same family.

Ancient Greece

The reincarnation concept was well known in ancient Greece.

The mathematician Pythagoras in the sixth century B.C. is said to have criticized a man beating a puppy: "Do not hit him; it is the soul of a friend of mine. I recognized it when I heard it cry out."

Pythagoras's statement suggests that humans can reincarnate as animals, an idea that probably originated in the Hindu religion. However, Sylvia Cranston and Carey Williams, in their book *Reincarnation*, write, "Today, Western reincarnationists affirm that 'once a human being, always a human being.'"

The Greek philosopher, Plato (fourth century B.C.), also spoke of reincarnation. In his dialogue *Phaedrus*, Plato says: "By making the right use of those things remembered from the former life, by constantly perfecting himself in the mysteries, a man becomes truly perfect." Plato suggests that people have the opportunity to improve through a series of different lives.

Hinduism

Some of the world's greatest religions also see reincarnation as a fact. They see it as assisting us in our lives.

Hinduism, a religion practiced in India, is the oldest religion in the world. It dates to 4000 B.C. However, reincarnation did not appear in Hindu scriptures until around the sixth century B.C.

Among those scriptures is the Bhagavad-Gita. This records a dialogue between Lord Krishna, one of India's spiritual teachers, and Arjuna, a warrior. Krishna instructs Arjuna on how to overcome his human limitations and be victorious on the battlefield. But Krishna's teachings have a double meaning for Arjuna.

Lord Krishna and Arjuna.

Arjuna's battlefield is really in his heart and soul—he must fight within himself to rise to perfection.

According to the Bhagavad-Gita, everybody goes through the cycle of life, death, and rebirth until they are enlightened—wise, perfect, and at one with creation: "As the dweller in this boy passed into childhood, youth and age, so also does he pass into another body. This does not bewilder the wise."

Who are the wise? Those who have become enlightened. They have broken the cycle of rebirth and do not have to return to this life. But as the Bhagavad-Gita suggests, until one has attained enlightenment, the Ferris wheel of life and death continues.

The Bhagavad-Gita offers an interesting description of the reincarnation process. When we die, we throw off our bodies like old clothes. When we reincarnate, we put on a new set of clothes, our new bodies!

Karma

Hinduism has a companion belief to reincarnation called *karma*. Karma means *action and the results*

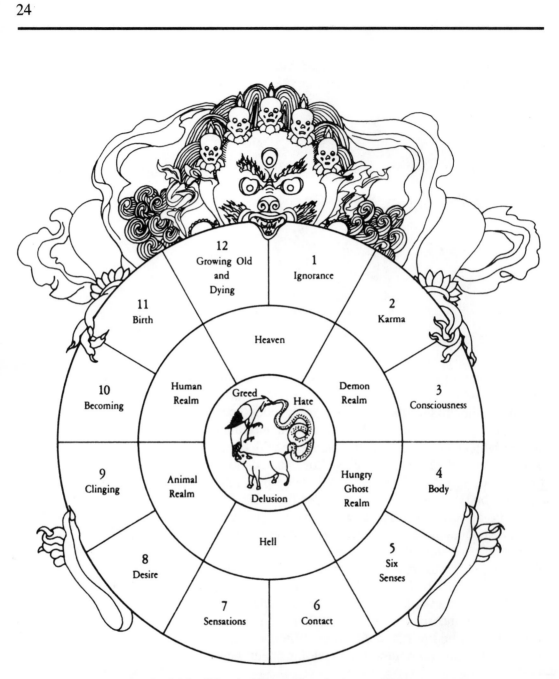

A version of the Buddhist *Wheel of Becoming*. It shows different states and distractions a person experiences before leaving material existence (life) and reaching perfection.

of action. The concept of karma suggests we may be either rewarded or punished for our actions in a previous life. Self-called witch Sybil Leek says that karma "is the fate we create for ourselves as a result of our actions in this and previous existences."

The "law" of karma apparently acts as a cosmic court of justice. How? Every action, according to the meaning of karma, has an effect. For example, suppose someone is visiting the beach. That person sees a woman drowning and saves her. Because of the karmic effects of this action, someone may someday save that person's life or he or she may be rewarded in some other way.

What if a thief steals a poor man's wallet containing his last twenty dollars? Someday someone may steal from that thief!

There is a saying in the Bible that is similar to the karma concept—as one plants, so shall one harvest. According to Hindu belief, what one sows shall come back lifetimes from now. The law of karma has no timetable. If reincarnation occurs, our actions could catch up with us. To illustrate, pretend you have moved from Ohio to Oregon and then to Florida. Your mail gets sent by the post office to you in Ohio, then forwarded to Oregon and Florida. It continues to be forwarded until it gets delivered to you. In the same way,

Scientists and our own experience tell us that for every action there is an equal and opposite reaction.

Hindus believe karma eventually catches up with us—a cosmic postal service!

Joe Fisher, in *The Case for Reincarnation*, writes that "karma has produced the present from the deeds of past lives, and prepares us for eternity through the actions of today." Each life depends on its previous one.

Modern physics has a concept similar to that of karma. It is the principle of cause and effect. For every action, there is an equal and opposite reaction. A rock thrown at a wall does not just stop; it bounces part way back. A friend who is slapped may slap back.

David Christie-Murray, in his book, *Reincarnation, Ancient Beliefs and Modern Evidence*, states that the Hindu reincarnationist believes "love at first sight, friendships, antipathies [dislikes], reflect relationships in a previous life."

Reincarnation, to the Hindu believer, means another chance for enlightenment. If we have had bad relationships in the past, they must be resolved. Karma suggests that we cannot escape ourselves and our problems.

Christianity

In another major religion, Christianity, belief in reincarnation has followed a different path.

Joe Fisher, in *The Case for Reincarnation*, argues that early Christians accepted the reincarnation doctrine. The concept was a fact of life to them. According to Fisher, the architect who structured the concept into early Christianity was Origen (A.D. 185-254). Origen was a theologian (a specialist in the study of God and religion) and one of the Church's most famous teachers. He wrote in his book *De Principiis*, "Every soul . . . comes into this world strengthened by the victories or weakened by the defeats of its previous life. Its place in this world as a vehicle appointed to honor or dishonor, is determined by its previous merits

> "Every soul . . . comes into this world strengthened by the victories or weakened by the defeats of its previous life."
>
> Early church teacher Origen

> "If anyone assert the fabulous pre-existence of souls, and shall assert the monstrous restoration which follows from it: let him be anathema."
>
> The Fifth Ecumenical Council, "The Anathemas Against Origen"

or demerits. Its work in this world determines its place in the world which is to follow.''

Does this sound like karma? Many early Christians subscribed to Origen's teaching. They embraced the doctrine of reincarnation until the sixth century A.D., by which time Christianity was an established institution.

However, Fisher explains, there was another Christian group who strictly interpreted the Biblical scriptures as meaning there was only one life. This faction, who controlled church policies, outlawed reincarnationist teachings in 593 at the Second Council of Constantinople. The Roman Emperor Justinian presided over the proceedings. He issued fourteen anathemas (curses), four of them directed against reincarnation. Justinian basically declared war against Origen's followers. Ever since, the official Christian Church has avoided the reincarnation doctrine.

Why did they shun the belief? Fisher suggests early reincarnationists preferred to guide their own lives without relying on established religions. They didn't need religious leaders to tell them how to live their lives. Hans Holzer, author of *Patterns of Destiny*, wrote, ''The Church needed the whip of judgment day to keep the faithful in line. It was, therefore, a matter of survival for the Church not to allow belief in reincarnation to take hold among her followers.''

Although talk of reincarnation was silenced, some Christian sects clung to their beliefs, notably the Cathars in Europe during the Middle Ages. The official Church, however, started a crusade of terror to extinguish the Cathars and other rebel groups. According to Fisher, reincarnational thinking had been uprooted from public awareness by the sixteenth century.

Today, more and more Christians believe in reincarnation. In a 1980 lecture, California theology professor Dr. Pascal Kaplan remarked that there is a growing number of ministers, nuns, and priests who

Origen, one of the Church's early teachers who believed in reincarnation.

Elijah taken up to heaven in a chariot of fire.

accept reincarnation. They believe that rebirth "promises a framework for a deeper, truer understanding of their religion and of the essence of Christian spirituality."

The Bible

Does the Bible speak of reincarnation? Joseph Head and Sylvia Cranston, in their book *Reincarnation in World Thought*, claim that it does. They cite Ecclesiastes 1:9-11 as suggesting reincarnation: "The thing that hath been, it is that which shall be . . . and there is no new thing under the sun. Is there anything thereof it may be said, See, this is new? It hath been already of old times, which was before me. There is no remembrance of former things."

Joe Fisher believes the idea of karma is clearly outlined in the Bible: "St. Paul's statement in his Epistle to the Galatians, ' . . . what soever a man soweth, that shall he also reap' (Galatians 6:7) hints strongly at rebirth because one life is plainly insufficient for a perfect balancing of accounts."

Do such references indicate a Christian acceptance of reincarnation? There is no agreement on this. Biblical passages can be interpreted differently. Joe Fisher says, "while the Old and New Testaments hardly trumpet the belief from the rooftops," their references to reincarnation confirm a longstanding Christian belief in it.

Many people throughout the world accept reincarnation. But is it more than a belief—is reincarnation a fact? Are there any tools which we can use to explore these questions?

Two

Can Hypnotism Tell Us About Past Lives?

What evidence do we have that reincarnation may be real? For one thing, people claim to remember past lives.

Ma Tin Aung Myo, of Na-Thul, Burma, began talking about her previous life when she was two or three years old. Every time an airplane flew overhead, the girl would cry and cower from it. She explained to her parents that she was afraid of getting shot.

Ma Tin Aung Myo believed she had been a Japanese soldier in World War II, and had been shot and killed by an Allied plane!

Reports of past lives come through several avenues. Most come from regressive hypnosis, spontaneous recall, dreams, visions, and déjà vu experiences (events that seem as familiar as if they have been experienced before). In this chapter, we will explore some possible evidence of reincarnation discovered through hypnotism.

Hypnotism has become an increasingly respected tool for investigating and healing disturbed minds. The hypnotist induces, or helps bring about, a relaxed, sleeplike state in the subject (the person being hypnotized). The hypnotist normally uses the rhythmic

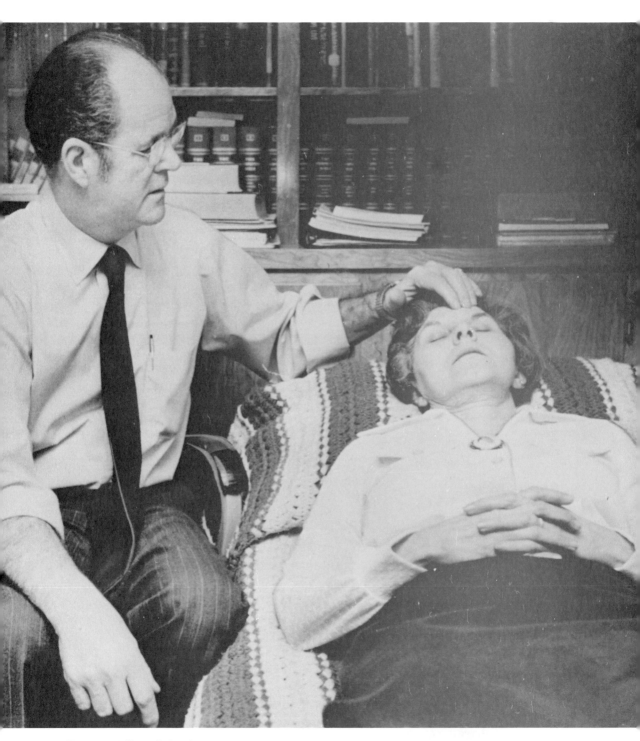

Reverend Carroll Jay induces a hypnotic trance in his wife, Dolores. Therapists of various kinds—from medical doctors and psychologists to those who try to end a client's bad habit of overeating, smoking, or nailbiting—use hypnotism to help their clients.

An old German cartoon gives an unflattering portrait of the hypnotist.

sound of his or her voice to suggest relaxation.

For example, the hypnotist may slowly count to twenty, suggesting that by the time the number twenty is reached, the subject will be totally relaxed. Once hypnotized, the subject responds to suggestions given by the hypnotist. For example, subjects may be told that they cannot raise their left arm. They will be surprised to find, that, indeed, they cannot raise their arm!

Ian Wilson, in his book *All in the Mind*, says that 80 percent of the population is hypnotizable. Hypnotism is often used to help people quit bad personal habits, such as smoking. It is also used as a form of therapy.

Some therapists claim hypnotism helps retrieve forgotten information about a patient's present-life experiences. Using hypnotherapy, a therapist can regress, or "send," a subject back in time—to when the subject was a teenager, a child, even a baby.

Some therapists also believe a subject's current life problems may result from past lives. Hypnotism, they believe, can help retrieve information from these past lives. For example, perhaps a person has a fear of heights. Did that person die from an accidental fall in a previous life? Therapists believe hypnosis may reveal the answer, which the patient can then learn to deal with.

During hypnosis, a patient may emotionally relive past experiences. Joe Fisher, in *The Case for Reincarnation*, writes,

A hearty-voiced plumber might become a lisping peasant girl, a placid secretary could take on the persona of a fierce warrior. . . .

However a past life is perceived, the aim of the therapy is to mine the experience of the soul; to heal through self-understanding.

By understanding our past, therapists believe, we can understand why we are the way we are in the present. This, in turn, will help direct our future experience of life.

The Case of Bridey Murphy

In 1956, the idea of reincarnation exploded across America following the publication of Morey Bernstein's book *The Search for Bridey Murphy*.

Virginia Tighe, a shy young woman who gained notoriety when "Bridey Murphy" was revealed to the world.

Bernstein, a Pueblo, Colorado, businessman and an amateur hypnotist, conducted a series of tape-recorded, hypnotic regressions. His subject was Virginia Tighe, called Ruth Simmons in the book. During the sessions, Tighe described a former life she lived in nineteenth-century Ireland. She claimed her name was Bridey Murphy.

A national best-seller, the book stirred such a heated controversy over reincarnation that news reporters extensively investigated the case. Two questions emerged from the case: Is reincarnation a fact? Does recall under hypnosis prove it?

D. Scott Rogo is a noted researcher in the field of parapsychology (the study of things that cannot be explained in usual ways, including ESP, ghosts, and other strange phenomena). In his book *The Search for Yesterday*, he explains that the Murphy case was impressive because of "how Virginia Tighe began recalling more and more obscure bits of information about Ireland and nineteenth-century Irish life as the sessions proceeded."

What were some of these details?

Virginia revealed that she lived in Cork in the early 1800s, and that her father was Duncan Murphy, an

Left: Morey Bernstein. Right: Bernstein and Virginia Tighe. He created a sensation when he hypnotized Virginia and then wrote a book called *The Search for Bridey Murphy.*

Irish lawyer. She further explained that her father was a Protestant and her mother's name was Kathleen. Bridey was born in 1798. She married the twenty-year-old son of another Cork barrister (lawyer), Brian Joseph McCarthy. The couple moved to Belfast. Brian went to school and later taught at Queen's University. Bridey claimed she died at sixty-six and was buried in Belfast in 1864.

Controversy About Bridey

Was Virginia Tighe really Bridey Murphy?

In such cases, historical research is invaluable. It can verify or discount the details brought out through hypnosis. D. Scott Rogo reports that "newspaper reporters, skeptics, and believers alike searched through both Mrs. Tighe's background as well as Irish history to discover the truth behind her memories."

According to Rogo, research did verify some of Tighe's statements. Other aspects of her story were doubted. For example, no birth records were ever found that proved the existence of Bridey Murphy, Duncan Murphy, Kathleen Murphy, or Brian Joseph McCarthy. However, Rogo adds, such reports do not date that far back in Ireland.

Was any evidence discovered that confirmed any of Tighe's claims? Perhaps. Rogo says that reporter William J. Barker's twelve-page article in the March 11, 1956, issue of the *Denver Post* "*partially* confirmed Mrs. Tighe's hypnotic claims."

Rogo summarizes part of Barker's article:

> During one of the later regressions, "Bridey" mentioned the names of two grocers from whom she bought food. The names were given as Farr's and John Carrigan. A search undertaken by Belfast's chief librarian at Barker's request documented that these gentlemen were listed in the city directory for 1865-6. They were, in fact, the only two grocers in business at the time. What Barker found even more impressive was that several statements "Bridey" had made during the regressions turned out to be true, even

"All of us are able to construct fantasies and do it with great regularity. Why is it that we would believe that fantasies constructed under hypnosis reflect actual past lives?"

Professor Nicholas S. Spanos, Carleton University, Canada

"They [scientists] may instinctively reject rebirth, because if it were true, a lifetime of research based on the theory that matter and energy are the only realities would be undermined."

Author Sylvia Cranston

Virginia Tighe, under hypnosis, was able to tell many details about nineteenth-century Ireland. Was this because she had lived there in a former life?

though experts on Irish life were skeptical of them. The most famous of these was "Bridey's" claim that her husband was a barrister. This seemed unlikely, since Catholics were not emancipated (given freedom) in Ireland until the 1820s and therefore couldn't have practiced law during the early years of "Bridey's" marriage. Barker was able to learn in Ireland, however, that a Catholic Relief Act was passed in 1793, which ruled that Catholics could enter the legal profession. "Bridey" also asserted that she lived in a house called "The Meadows." Barker was able to dig up a map of County Cork dating back to 1801, and while no house by that name could be traced, there was an area in Cork known by that bucolic [rural] designation.

Rogo believes some of Tighe's information was so detailed it presented evidence for reincarnation. The reporter Barker remained neutral in the case. Other people did not.

According to Rogo, the most severe criticism of the case appeared in a series of articles printed by the *Chicago American* in May and June of 1956. The reports stated that Tighe, as a child, lived with an Irish aunt, Marie Burns. The aunt told Virginia Tighe stories of her native country. Hence, Tighe's reincarnation memories may actually have been distorted memories from her present life.

Did Tighe confuse her own childhood with an apparent past life? William Barker, the *Denver Post* reporter, continued to study the case. He found that Marie Burns actually grew up in New York, not Ireland. Thus, possibly Tighe wasn't confusing her childhood with a past life.

Rogo discusses another reported claim against Tighe's story, one that held up.

It was reported that an Irish woman named Mrs. Anthony Bridie Murphy Corkell (the alleged model for Mrs. Tighe's "Bridey Murphy" of County Cork) had once lived across the street from Virginia Tighe's aunt and uncle. Barker looked into the matter and was able to locate the basis of the story. It was true that she had once lived near Mrs. Tighe's relatives, but he could not document that her maiden name was Murphy. On the other hand, he did discover that Bridey Murphy was a rather common [name] in Chicago. The reporter also checked out Mrs. Corkell's background and found that she had lived in an area

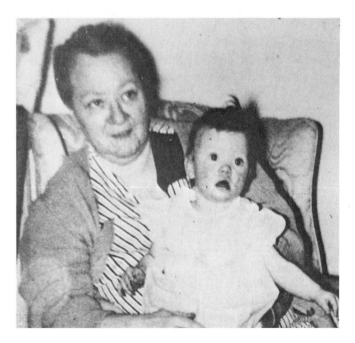

Mrs. Bridie Murphy Corkell. Was there an important connection between her and Virginia Tighe?

miles away from where "Bridey" and her husband purportedly lived.

Was the Irish woman Corkell the source of Tighe's memories? Probably not, if Barker's research is accurate.

Helen Wambach

Dr. Helen Wambach, a psychiatrist and past-life therapist, has explored past-life recall through hypnosis. In her book *Reliving Past Lives*, she recounts the hypnotic regressions of many of her subjects. "Mark" is one of them. Before consulting Wambach, he had visited Europe. Traveling through northern Italy, he had driven up a hill and passed a small stone building. It seemed familiar to him and Mark felt sad.

Wambach hypnotized Mark to explore the possibility of his having lived in Italy in a past life. She regressed him to the year 1600, then to 1450. The following are excerpts from that recorded session.

W: Now you are drifting peacefully along. You feel very easy and relaxed. You are floating backward through time. It is the year 1600. Do you see anything?

M: Just faces drifting along. No, don't really see anything, just misty haze.

W: We are going back through time again. It is the year 1450. Do you see anything?

M: A hill. I'm riding and I see the hills and trees.

W: What do you see around you?

M: I'm coming up to a large fort or building. I guess it's a castle . . . it's my castle . . . it isn't really very big.

W: How old are you?

M: Don't know. I'm a man . . .

W: Are there any people around you?

M: I have my men with me. We're going into the castle.

W: One of the men calls you by your name. What does he call you?

M: I think it's . . . Graf something.

W: These men, do they work with you?

M: We are fighting. They fight with me.

W: Who are you fighting for?

M: The Holy Roman Emperor.

Wambach further reports Mark said he had been a knight in that life. He said he died in the castle after a lonely and hard life.

What Mark described under hypnosis is what Dr. Ian Stevenson, the world's leading authority on the evidence for reincarnation, calls the informational aspect of reincarnation. People provide information about a past life. Then, to confirm whether such information might indicate reincarnation, the information must be researched and checked. With Mark's account, Wambach did just that.

Upon investigating Mark's claims, Wambach concluded he might have lived before! Wambach summarizes her investigations:

> The life of the Italian knight offered me only a few bits of data to check. He had said that his life was that of "Graf" and I checked this. This was a title that meant "Lord," and is of Germanic origin; but "Graf" is too widely understood for Mark's usage to prove any recall experience.
>
> The place in Italy he described to me appeared to be on the borders of what is now Austria. In 1450, there was an entirely different map of Europe. What puzzled me most was the description of fighting for the "Holy Roman Emperor." On checking, there does seem to be some evidence that this was the term used at that time.

A young Italian knight from the fifteenth century. Did Helen Wambach's subject, "Mark," really live a past life in medieval Italy?

In Wambach's study on past lives, she purposely asked her subjects for detailed information they could not have read or heard about. For example, Wambach inquired about landscapes and climate.

She also asked for personal descriptions and descriptions of utensils, clothing, and money used. Such information provided her with details that might be historically or archaeologically checked. If they were accurate, reincarnation might be indicated. Of

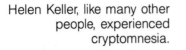

Helen Keller, like many other people, experienced cryptomnesia.

the one thousand subjects she regressed, half gave details that could be verified!

Cryptomnesia

Cryptomnesia, memories we are not consciously aware of, is an alternative explanation for past-life recall during hypnosis. Could "forgotten" memories of past incidents in one's present life suddenly emerge during hypnosis?

Helen Keller records an example of cryptomnesia in her autobiography, *The Story of My Life*. When she was a teenager, Helen wrote a short story that was published. However, she later discovered that aspects of her story were similar to those in a story published by Margaret T. Camby in her book *Birdie and His Fairy Friends*. Camby's book was published in 1874,

One of Reina Kampman's subjects claimed to have lived a former life as an innkeeper's daughter in thirteenth-century England. Her knowledge of medieval England was astonishing.

before Helen was born. Helen apparently had read the book when she was a child and unconsciously used features of Camby's plot as her own.

Skeptic Dr. Reina Kampman, a Finnish psychiatrist, questions reincarnation. He believes that reincarnation claims are based on cryptomnesia or on fantasies built around a severely disturbing event suffered in a patient's life.

In one of Kampman's hypnotic research projects, his nineteen-year-old subject claimed a life in thirteenth-century England. In this previous life, she said, her name was Dorothy and she was the daughter of an innkeeper. The subject described in detail English life of the time. What is more, she startled Kampman by singing an old folk song in the Middle English language.

Was this an instance of reincarnation or of cryptomnesia?

Kampman decided it was cryptomnesia. Several years after his research with this subject, he rehypnotized the girl. He asked her to trace the source of her information for the old English song.

D. Scott Rogo quotes Kampman's comments:

"She went back to the age of thirteen, when she once by chance took a book in her hand in the library. She did not read it but only ran through the pages. In hypnosis, she was able to tell the authors of the book, who were Benjamin Britten and [Gustav] Holst (music composers)."

Kampman found the book existed. It contained the very song his subject recited during hypnosis years before!

Does Kampman's research disprove reincarnation? Rogo answers no. Although Kampman's studies, says Rogo, "throw cold water on those believers and psychologists eager to find proof of reincarnation," Kampman's studies cannot explain other well-documented cases.

Kampman apparently only uncovered a few cases of genuine cryptomnesia, according to Rogo. "He had to cast his net in a sea of cut glass before pulling in a few gems. Cryptomnesia may be a phenomenon just as rare as genuine past-life memories."

Rogo thinks cryptomnesia is as difficult to prove as reincarnation is. A researcher must show that "the subject somehow gained access to information about [a claim]."

Still, Rogo cautions, "the historical information offered by some regressed subjects cannot constitute strong evidence for reincarnation. . . . This is just the type of data that anyone might pick up over the years but might consciously forget." The human mind, says Rogo, can register and file any sort of trivial information and then draw upon it in amazing ways during hypnotic regression.

Still, Rogo believes that to assume that reincarnation subjects could have come across much of the obscure information they give would be illogical. Researchers themselves have an uphill battle documenting names and dates that occur in reincarnation claims. This can result from language and cultural barriers and from lack of records such as dates of birth, marriage, and death. If professional researchers have this difficulty, how would ordinary people come across such information?

Fantasy

Another explanation sometimes given for the reincarnation stories people tell while hypnotized is that they are based on the subjects' fantasies. Under hypnosis, subjects may imaginatively make up stories. These are then accepted as clues to "hidden selves."

Nicholas P. Spanos, a professor in the Department of Psychology at Carleton University in Ottawa, Canada, thinks that hypnotic subjects can be led to develop the idea of these hidden selves. In an article in *The Skeptical Enquirer*, Spanos writes that in a number of studies, "many subjects behaved as if they possessed secondary selves that had experiences that differed from those of their 'normal selves'."

But, according to Spanos, research indicated that the hidden self is really a "performance." Imaginative

Above: New Jersey hypnotist Frank Lodato puts a client in a trance. Opposite page, top: Ray Bryant, an English journalist, seeks his own grave from a former life. Opposite page, below: Bryant is being "regressed" to a former life as Colour Sgt. Reuben Stafford who served in the Crimean War in the mid-1800s. While in a hypnotic trance, Bryant showed remarkable knowledge of the day-to-day progress of the campaign. The man on the right, Colonel Bird, is an expert on the war and questioned Bryant. He was impressed with Bryant's knowledge.

"Reincarnation party" at West Covina, California. The guests were supposed to come dressed as one of their former lives. Top, the invitation. Middle, the hostess, "Queen Isabella." Bottom, some of the guests.

Queen Isabella
(Spain ~ Fifteenth Century)
Invites you to a ~
"Come As You Were
Party ~

A Reincarnation Extravagan
February 18, 1984
Granada Royale
West Covina,
California

subjects "create the experiences and role behaviors called for by the instructions they are given. By varying the instructions, subjects can be easily led to develop 'hidden selves' with whatever characteristics the experimenters wish." In other words, either consciously or unconsciously, the hypnotist gives the subjects enough clues to construct a false past life.

Another reincarnation skeptic, Ian Wilson, in his book *All in the Mind*, suggests that past lives are based on "scripts" that are "provided by present-life material so deeply buried in the subject's brain that he or she will not have the slightest awareness of it." Thus, the fantasy lives are based on experiences deeply buried or forgotten but nevertheless part of the subject's current lifetime.

Dr. Edith Fiore, author of *You Have Been Here Before*, does not agree. She writes, "Are they putting on an act? If so, most should be nominated for Academy Awards. I have listened to and watched people in past-life regressions under hypnosis for thousands of hours. I am convinced there is no deliberate, no conscious, attempt to deceive. The tears, shaking, flinching, smiling, gasping for breath, groaning, sweating, and other physical manifestations are all too real."

Nor would Helen Wambach agree with the fantasy theory. Although cryptomnesia and fantasizing may explain some informational aspects of recall, she says, it does not explain their emotional content. Wambach writes, "For many hypnotic subjects, it is the emotional level of the experience that had meaning rather than its intellectual content."

This emotional aspect is particularly true of Wambach's subjects who, under hypnosis, experienced their deaths in past lives. "The emotions that my subjects experienced," says Wambach, "were so strong that they were reflected in their here-and-now bodies. One of the subjects reported, 'I could feel the tears trickling down my cheeks in the here-and-now, but

"The credibility of the 'past lives' of hypnotic regression subjects turns on the wealth of detail which they provide and which apparently they could not possibly have known by normal means."

Authors John Fairley & Simon Welfare, *Arthur C. Clarke's World of Strange Powers*

"Although widely exploited by lay hypnotists and even by a few psychologists who should know better, hypnotic regression to 'previous lives' (with rare exceptions) generates only fantasies."

Dr. Ian Stevenson, renowned reincarnation researcher

Smoke from aerial bombing of London during World War II. Dr. Helen Wambach found that many of her subjects who claimed to have lived previous lives during this time said they died of smoke inhalation—not an unusual kind of death during the war.

my whole body felt so light right after I died.'''

Wambach reports that about 10 percent of her subjects felt upset or sorrowful at death. They also expressed surprise at being outside their bodies and tried to remain near their loved ones.

Wambach's research includes statistics of violent deaths in past lives. According to her, the greatest number of deaths in her subjects happened in two time periods, 1000 B.C. and the twentieth century A.D. Many of her subjects found they died in minor wars around 1000 B.C. Wambach found the highest percentage (31 percent) of deaths in the 1900s resulted from bombings.

Her bombing subjects reported dying from smoke inhalation. According to Wambach, "this corresponds with facts regarding the bombing raids in World War II." Apparently more victims died from smoke inhalation than actual explosions. Wambach says this "is one of those small details it is unlikely my subjects would fantasize about."

Are past-life subjects all good actors—Marlon Brandos and Meryl Streeps?

Wambach thinks not. She states that her subjects strongly tend to tell the truth under hypnosis—they are not merely trying to please the hypnotist.

Moreover, she writes, ''If my subjects were fantasizing, their fantasies were bleak and barren. The great majority of my subjects went through their lives wearing rough homespun garments, living in crude huts, eating bland cereal grain with their fingers from wooden bowls.'' If they were fantasizing, why would they choose such dull lives to recall?

Wambach points out that ''a frequent objection to past-life recall is that so many people seemed to have been Cleopatra or high priests in Egypt in past lives.'' However, in the 1,088 cases Wambach researched, upper-class lives were less than 10 percent in each time period she measured. Between 60 and 77 percent of all the past lives she studied fell into the lower classes. ''None of my subjects reported a past life as a historical personage,'' Wambach says. Those who recall upper-class lives made comments like, ''That was a difficult life because I had so many respon-

One of the questions put by many skeptics of reincarnation is Why do so many people claim to have been famous persons like Cleopatra? (right) Why were there not more common people like the vineyard pickers? (left) In reality, there were many more peasants than royalty.

sibilities.''

The happiest lives, Wambach reports, were those lived as peasants or primitives.

Extrasensory Perception (ESP)

Extrasensory perception, or ESP, occurs when the mind receives information about an object, place, or time without perceiving that information through regular channels—our senses. Normal perception occurs when we take in information from our hearing, seeing, smelling, touching, and tasting senses.

Can ESP account for reincarnation claims during hypnosis?

D. Scott Rogo believes it is possible, but he has only found one case where ESP accounted for a past-life recall. In *The Search for Yesterday*, Rogo reports that in 1975 Dr. Dell Leonardi, a psychologist and hypnotist in Kansas City, Missouri, discovered a patient who seemed to be the reincarnation of John Wilkes Booth. (Booth assassinated President Abraham Lincoln.)

Some skeptics believe that hypnotists may unconsciously send information about the past into their subjects' minds with ESP.

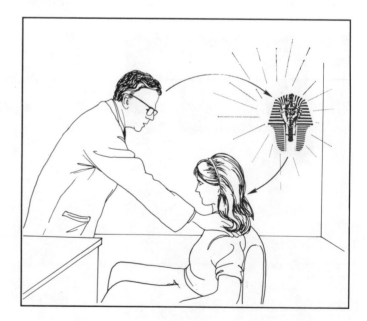

While Leonardi regressed one of her subjects, a college student, the man produced factual and obscure information about Booth. However, Leonardi had been reading about Booth at the time and realized that her subject "recalled" information about Booth that she herself had only recently discovered.

According to Rogo, "This certainly indicated the psychologist was 'leaking' information to the subject telepathically." In other words, perhaps the psychologist and the subject experienced telepathy, or mind-to-mind communication. The subject picked up on information in the psychologist's mind.

Writer David Christie-Murray, in his book, *Reincarnation*, agrees that telepathy can occur between hypnotist and subject. Moreover, he writes, a "hypnotized subject can telepathically locate distant persons with relevant pieces of information . . . and use all of this information imaginatively." The subjects could telepathically gather information from unknown persons, books, and statistical records and then shuf-

Above left, a man reads the Akashic records, a mysterious cosmic description of everything that goes on in the universe. Immediately above, Edgar Cayce, the mystic who described the Akashic records and claimed to have read from them.

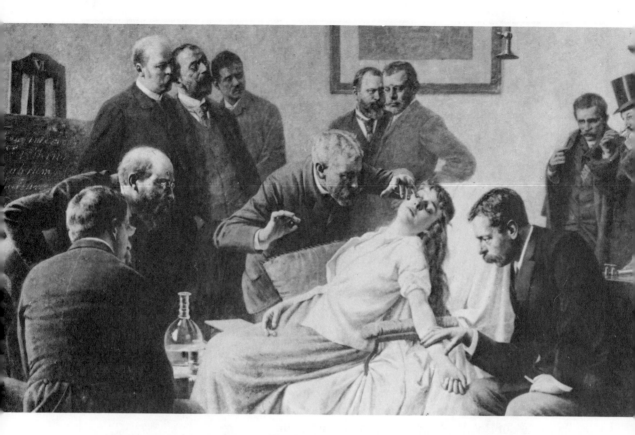

An experiment in hypnotism. Late nineteenth-century doctors hypnotize a patient.

fle the information together like a deck of cards and come up with imagined reincarnation stories.

Akashic Records

Some people think hypnotized subjects could be tapping into a universal memory bank, a subconscious worldwide field where everyone's memories are somehow deposited. According to psychics and mediums, people who practice ESP, there exists an invisible record, only available through ESP, in which is recorded everything that has occurred in the universe. It is called the Akashic Records. It supposedly contains the details of every human life.

Sylvia Cranston and Carey Williams write in their book, *Reincarnation*, about Edgar Cayce, the late psychic who gave past-life readings. Cayce once claimed that his source of information was not only his own subconscious mind but also the Akashic

Records. Cayce said the records were ''to the mental world as the cinema is to the physical world.'' In other words, through ESP, the Akashic Records could be viewed almost like a film.

Do hypnotized subjects have access to these records, if they exist? Do they view their own past lives or the lives of other people? How would they tell the difference?

As we have seen, hypnosis is one way through which reincarnation claims come. Are they true? We don't know.

However, such claims do emerge in other ways. Unlike hypnosis where people have to be hypnotized to remember past lives, spontaneous recall happens when people simply remember past lives while they are in a normal state of activity.

Three

Is Spontaneous Recall Proof of Reincarnation?

D. Scott Rogo remarks that people in all walks of life sometimes remember pieces of their past lives and that these moments can happen to anyone at any time. This is spontaneous recall. "Even people who have never heard about reincarnation report this," Rogo says.

Such cases are reported from around the world. Many come from young children whose memories of past lives are quite intact.

Since 1960, Dr. Ian Stevenson, Carlson Professor of Psychiatry and Director of the Division of Personality Studies at the University of Virginia, has been researching spontaneous recall claims of former lives. Stevenson has documented nearly two thousand cases in India, Africa, the Near and Far East, Britain, the United States, and other countries. Most of the cases have focused on children.

Of his work, Stevenson says in an *Omni* magazine interview that he has many examples of "such things as early childhood phobias [fears], . . . uncanny abilities that seem to develop spontaneously, . . . children convinced they are the wrong sex, [and] congenital [birth] deformities." Some of these cases "cannot be

Opposite: Why is it that more young children than adults are likely to experience spontaneous recall of former lives?

Ian Stevenson, famous reincarnation researcher.

satisfactorily explained by genetics, environmental influences, or a combination of these.''

Why does Stevenson study children and rarely adults? To avoid the possibility of cryptomnesia. In the *Omni* magazine interview, Stevenson states: "Obviously children are too young to have absorbed a great deal of information, especially about deceased people in some distant town. In better cases, they couldn't have known about them.''

According to Stevenson, the age at which a child will speak of a past life is from about two or three to five years old. "I cannot emphasize too strongly that a child who is going to remember a previous life has only about three years in which he will talk about it. Before the age of two or three he lacks the ability. After five, too much else will be happening in his life, and he will begin to forget.''

Patterns

Moreover, Stevenson believes children may demonstrate patterns they developed in other lives since they are too young to have developed them in their present lives.

According to Stevenson in his book *Twenty Cases Suggestive of Reincarnation*, "one solution to the question of survival [reincarnation] lies in the observation of 'patterns' within one personality or organism which . . . could not have been inherited or acquired in the present life of that personality.''

What are these patterns?

Some of the behavioral similarities Stevenson looks for in his research are these:

- verbal expressions used by the person identified as the former life;
- repeated presentation of information about the previous personality coming in the form of memories of events experienced or of people already known;
- requests to go to the previous home;
- familiar address and behavior toward people related to the previous personality;
- emotional responses such as likes and dislikes;
- mannerisms, habits, and skills . . . appropriate for the previous personality.

Marta Lorenz

Stevenson cites the case of Brazilian Marta Lorenz as an example. Marta was born August 14, 1918, to Ida Lorenz.

Marta Lorenz had many things in common with her mother's deceased friend, Sinhá.

"Children born with deformed limbs—or even without fingers, toes and hands—have claimed to remember being murdered and state that the murderer had removed these fingers, toes, or hands during the killing."

Reincarnation researcher Ian Stevenson

"Does our subconscious produce past life impressions from scraps of our current life, in the way it creates our dreams? Or do these reincarnation memories under hypnosis reflect the real past?"

Author and reincarnation researcher Helen Wambach

When Marta was two-and-a-half years old, she began commenting about her previous life as Sinhá. Sinhá died at twenty-seven years of age in October 1917, of tuberculosis. She had promised her good friend, Ida Lorenz, she would reincarnate as Ida's daughter.

Prior to Sinhá's death, she had fallen in love with two men, both of whom her father disapproved. One man committed suicide and Sinhá fell into a state of depression. She wanted to die. Neglecting her health, she purposely tried to catch cold and exhaust herself. Her larynx, or "voice box," became infected and the infection spread to her lungs. On her deathbed, her voice was so hoarse she could barely whisper.

According to Stevenson, Ida's daughter Marta spontaneously spoke of Sinhá's life and acquaintances on more than 120 occasions. Stevenson was able to record and verify 28 of Marta's declarations.

What similarities did Stevenson discover between Marta and Sinhá?

- Both were fond of cats.
- Both enjoyed dancing.
- Sinhá had wanted an education. Marta wanted to become a teacher and became one.
- Both feared rain.
- Both feared blood.
- Sinhá indirectly committed suicide. Marta, throughout her life, often wanted to die.

Moreover, Stevenson writes, both had more than average powers of extrasensory perception. For instance, Sinhá had often announced ahead of time that her friend Ida Lorenz was coming to visit the family. Marta's grandmother once gave her a book on reincarnation. Marta wouldn't take it, saying, according to Stevenson, "The book is about a case similar to mine."

Does Marta's case offer proof of reincarnation?

Both Marta and Sinha loved cats. With other similarities, was this evidence of reincarnation?

Stevenson explains that extrasensory perception might account for Marta's information about Sinhá. She might have learned about Sinhá through the thoughts of her mother, Ida. However, he does not think an ESP theory can account for the behavioral similarities. How would ESP explain their similar fears, likes, and activities?

Stevenson does admit that some behavioral features may merely resemble a previous personality's and not be proof of reincarnation. Some of Marta's behavior that was similar to Sinhá's may simply have been coincidence.

Is there other behavioral evidence pointing to reincarnation? What if someone spoke in a foreign language, old and no longer in use?

Xenoglossy

Xenoglossy means the revival of a forgotten, or dead, language. Sometimes this occurs in reincarnation cases.

D. Scott Rogo, in *The Search for Yesterday*, says of language: "We learn it by practice, and one cannot master a technical skill without this practice. One skill we all learn during the course of our lives is language. If a person could recall and correctly use

D. Scott Rogo, author of books about reincarnation.

a language he or she allegedly spoke during a past life, this would be considered valid evidence of reincarnation.''

Although cases of xenoglossy are rare, Rogo tells about a classic one, the case of ''Rosemary.''

Dr. F. H. Wood was a British organist and musicologist (one who studies music). In 1927, he met Miss Ivy Carter Beaumont, a psychic medium (a person who acts as channel of communication between the earthly and spirit worlds). Beaumont was also known as ''Rosemary.'' According to Rogo, Wood hoped to ''find evidence proving the survival of the soul.'' He took interest in Rosemary who, in trance states, was apparently relaying messages from ancient Egypt. Not only did she speak in an ancient Egyptian language, but she also recalled a past life along the Nile River. By 1940, says Rogo, Wood had compiled three notebooks on the Rosemary case and had collected five thousand phrases of ancient Egyptian!

What Wood discovered was someone—Lady Nona —communicating through Rosemary. Lady Nona was

Someone called "Lady Nona" supposedly spoke through the medium Ivy
Carter Beaumont. She was able to give many details of life in ancient Egypt.

"In the present state of parapsychological research, the hypothesis of rebirth in its various formulations (and by implication *all* survival of human personality after death) remains untestable."

Biologist and psychologist C.T.K. Chari

"It is perfectly normal for people to remember past lives. Nearly everyone can do it. You don't have to be Bridey Murphy or a psychic."

Reincarnation researcher Helen Wambach

a friend of Rosemary's in a past life. At first, Rosemary told of ancient Egypt in modern English. Then an Egyptologist (one who studies ancient Egypt) was brought in. Alfred J. Howard Hulme asked Wood whether Lady Nona could deliver messages in the ancient language. This would help validate Rosemary's statements and give more information about the language itself.

Three months after Hulme's request, Lady Nona spoke through Rosemary at the end of a session. She said, "Ah-ýit-as-zhúla." Hulme approximated the sound of the phrase to the written language and came up with the translation, "Saluted art thou, at the end."

Hulme believed the language spoken by Rosemary dated from between 2400 and 1356 B.C. In 1937, Wood and Hulme published a book analyzing the linguistic aspects of this language. In the book, *Ancient Egypt Speaks*, they concluded that Rosemary used correct grammar and vocabulary in the long-forgotten tongue.

Is the Rosemary case evidence for life after death and reincarnation? Not everyone thinks so.

Egyptologist?

Rogo points out that some critics think Hulme was not an expert in the language as he claimed. Hulme's research was attacked in 1937 by Professor Battiscombe Gunn, an Egyptologist at Oxford University. Gunn stated that Hulme probably read the wrong meanings into Lady Nona's utterances and then tampered with the linguistic phrases to make them fit Egyptian vocabulary.

A more recent critic, Ian Wilson, in his book *All in the Mind*, questions Hulme's background as an Egyptologist. Wilson took the Rosemary records to another Egyptologist, John Ray at Cambridge University. Ray concluded that Hulme's understanding of the language was flawed.

According to Rogo, Ray found that Hulme had erred in his grammatical research and confused the language with a later Egyptian language.

Criticism aside, Rogo says what is impressive is not that Rosemary's language was perfect, "but that the medium came out with anything resembling Egyptian at all."

Had Rosemary lived before? Was Lady Nona really a friend or was she actually Rosemary remembering a language from a past life? Controversy over this question remains.

Not only could Lady Nona tell about Egypt; she could speak in an ancient Egyptian language.

The Case of Mishra

There are other reported cases of xenoglossy. Ian Stevenson tells about a little girl named Swarnlata Mishra who lived in an Indian province where Hindu was the native language.

Sometimes, Mishra would dance and sing. Her singing was in Bengali, a different Indian language. The songs were based on poems written by Rabindranath Tagore, a famous Indian poet. Mishra said she learned the dances and songs in a previous life in the Bengalese city of Sylhet.

Was Mishra once a dancer and singer, or had she simply learned these things in her present lifetime?

D. Scott Rogo in *The Search for Yesterday* says it cannot be ruled out "that the girl had, at some time unknown to her parents, learned the songs from records." Moreover, Rogo states that in xenoglossic cases, children may easily have heard other languages during their early years. "All of us have ample opportunity to learn bits and phrases of several foreign languages." For example, he writes, "It is not rare

These two little girls, sisters from Sri Lanka, claimed to recall former lives. Their families supported their claims, saying the girls knew many things they could not have known in any other way.

to hear Italian spoken in Brazil, just as it is not odd to hear Greek spoken in New York or Russian in San Francisco."

Can xenoglossy, then, still be used as evidence for reincarnation? Or is it too unreliable? Even the experts disagree on this. However, Ian Stevenson investigated and published an article about a favorable xenoglossic case in the 1970s. He worked with Dr. Satwant Pasrica, an Indian psychologist, on the case of Uttara Huddar.

Uttara was a young woman about thirty-three years of age living in Nagpur in western India. Occasionally, Uttara would fall into trances, during which she would speak the Bengali language. Uttara supposedly knew only Marathi.

In addition, Uttara seemed to be familiar with early nineteenth-century Bengal. She knew its customs and mentioned names from "her" family there. Uttara had never visited Bengal; Nagpur was hundreds of miles away.

In December 1973, Uttara became ill. She was hospitalized for blackouts and headaches. During her hospitalization, she would awaken from sleep, claiming to be Sharada, a Bengali woman who lived in the nineteenth century!

Between 1974 and April 1977, Uttara apparently became Sharada twenty-three times. She would appear unaware of Uttara and did not know the Huddar family. Such periods sometimes lasted more than a week.

Was Uttara reliving a past life, remembering her old language? Was this a case of multiple personality?

Rogo notes that Sharada seemed unaware she was dead: ''Her last memory is that she fell unconscious (and presumably died) from a snakebite.'' Furthermore, Rogo writes that ''she has mentioned the proper names of scores of her relatives and has revealed a wealth of geographical and historical facts about Bengal.'' Eighty-five to be exact, all documented and verified by investigators!

Drs. Stevenson and Pasrica meticulously examined the historical details that came from Sharada. They were then able to construct a genealogy, or family tree, of Sharada's Bengali life. Her family name was Chattopadhaya. Stevenson and Pasrica located the head of the Chattopadhaya family in Bengal. He verified some

Uttara Huddar fell into spontaneous trances during which she believed she was Sharada, a Bengali woman from the past century.

It is not unusual to see people from different cultures, to hear different languages, and to be exposed to other customs in any large city.

of the names in the family tree and Sharada's relationship to them.

Stevenson reported to the American Society for Psychical Research that "the correspondence between the genealogy and her statements about the relationships of the male members of the family seems beyond coincidence."

Stevenson also discovered Uttara had a fear of snakes as a child. Sharada claimed her last conscious memory was of being bitten by a snake! Rogo asks: "Could it be merely coincidence that, while she was pregnant, Uttara's mother *had recurrent dreams of being bitten in the foot by a snake*? Perhaps in some strange way, Uttara Huddar's mother was already being told just 'who' her daughter *really* was even before her birth."

Rogo writes that Sharada's command of the Bengali language has been documented—she speaks fluent Bengali. Yet Uttara does not. If not reincarnation, what can explain this case?

Drs. Stevenson and Pasrica concluded that "Sharada is a discarnate personality—that is, that she consists of surviving aspects of a real person who lived and died in the early years of the nineteenth century."

Spontaneous recall may or may not point to reincarnation. But what about remarkable talents that could not have come from a person's parents? What about birthmarks that look exactly like scars or marks on a deceased person? Might these be evidence of reincarnation?

"Sharada" may have died of a snakebite; while pregnant with Uttara, her mother dreamt of being bitten by a snake; Uttara feared snakes. Do all of these coincidences mean that Uttara really was the reincarnation of Sharada?

Four

Special Skills and Birth Marks—The Solution?

Some people believe that special skills learned in one life might be carried over to another. Are some people naturally talented in one area of interest, or does this talent pass from one life, where it was developed, to the next?

Ian Stevenson, in *Twenty Cases*, reports the case of Paulo Lorenz who may have been the reincarnation of his dead sister Emilia.

What is unusual and what interests Stevenson about Paulo was his talent for sewing. Out of thirteen children in the Lorenz family, only Paulo and Emilia had highly developed sewing skills.

Stevenson's research showed that years before her death, Emilia said that if reincarnation existed, she would return as a man. She died on October 12, 1921.

Paulo was born February 3, 1923. He refused to wear boys' clothes until he was about six. He wore girls' clothes and played with dolls. Like Emilia before him, he showed a talent for sewing before he was five—without instruction.

How could Paulo have learned to sew?

Genetics

Some people believe that the genetic transmission

Opposite: Many children are born with birthmarks of one kind or another. The older girl in this picture has birthmarks on her fingers. Can such marks provide evidence of reincarnation if they are identical to the marks a deceased person had?

Wolfgang Mozart, musical prodigy. Did his genius come from a past life, or was it a special gift of his own?

of information from one generation to another accounts for reincarnation claims. Science knows that genetic codes, or blueprints, in every cell of our bodies contain the information needed to reproduce a new human being. Does this explain why someone is born a genius? Was Paulo Lorenz talented at sewing because it was embedded in his genetic background?

Sylvia Cranston and Carey Williams, in their book *Reincarnation*, note that musical geniuses Mozart, Bach, Beethoven, and Brahms all came from musically-inclined families. The authors say "genetic factors could explain their powers." But what about composer Handel, who was not from a musical family?

Cranston and Williams tell the story of a young genius in whom heredity does not seem to be a factor. Shakuntala Devi was born in India. She confounds people with her ability to solve mathematical problems faster than any machine.

According to Cranston and Williams, in 1977 Devi outperformed one of the world's most advanced computers, a Univac 1108. Devi figured out the twenty-third root of a 201-digit number in less than fifty seconds, faster than the computer!

Devi's mathematical talent was discovered when she was three years old. Even then she could work out logarithms, roots, and sums in minutes.

Moreover, she had little education and her parents had no skills with numbers. It certainly could not be genetics that gave Devi her talent. Was it reincarnation?

According to Cranston and Williams, Devi explained in an interview that she believed reincarnation was the source of her talent. She also suggested that she recalled a past life in Egypt.

Cranston and Williams point out that "it cannot be denied that there were once extraordinary mathematicians in the land of the Pharaohs."

In her book *Immortality and Human Destiny*, Sylvia Cranston asks: "Is genius the product of a for-

Shakuntala Devi is shown sitting onstage at a Texas university where she demonstrated her ability to out-compute a Univac computer. It took her fifty seconds to figure out the twenty-third root of a 201-digit number; it took the computer more than a minute. A math professor used up more than four minutes simply writing the answer on the board. Where did Shakuntala get such an exceptional talent?

> "Birth is not a beginning; death is not an end. There is existence without limitation; there is continuity without a starting point."
>
> Chuang Tzu, Chinese mystic

> "We should accept theories including survival of the personality after physical death only when theories along normal lines . . . fail to account for all the facts of a case."
>
> Scientist Ian Stevenson

tuitous [chance] combination of genes? Is it a gift of God, who has special favorites among us? Or is it more logical to think that it is the product of experience—of many lives?"

In his *Twenty Cases*, Stevenson writes that genetic transmission might explain a skill recurring in the same family. However, as in the case of Paulo, such a theory does not explain how a skill may occur in two children in the same family but not in the other children.

Stevenson states that although genetics may account for similarities between family members, "reincarnation may account for the differences."

Chang and Eng

Joe Fisher, in his book *The Case for Reincarnation*, states that the "most popular argument against reincarnation as the source of precocious talent is the theory that memory is genetically transferred from generation to generation." People with special talents "somehow dip into this genetic material . . . to draw on a skill well developed in an ancestor," Fisher says.

Fisher would agree with Stevenson—heredity might account for similarities, but not for differences. For example, Fisher writes of Siamese twins Chang and Eng. Siamese twins come from the same ovum, or egg cell, which begins to divide into twin cells but never completes the division. Because of this, Siamese twins are fused together when they are born. It would be natural to assume that such twins would be very like each other both physically and in personality. But did Chang and Eng develop similar personalities, genetically inherited? No, according to Fisher. For one thing, Chang loved alcohol and drinking. Eng never drank. This provided some evidence that genetics does not explain people's behavior. But does it prove that *reincarnation* explains people's behavior?

Physical Patterns

There is another pattern in the reincarnation mys-

tery. In his studies, Stevenson has traced the appearance of birthmarks, and sometimes scars, wounds, and even birth defects in his subjects.

In Stevenson's *Omni* magazine interview, he states: "I've reported on a case of a child who claimed to have been his own paternal grandfather and had two pigmented moles in the same spots on his body that his grandfather did. It's said in such instances that genetics is responsible. But one wonders why the one grandchild in ten who had the moles claimed to remember his grandfather's life."

Let us examine one of the more impressive birthmark cases Stevenson presents in his *Twenty Cases*.

Chang and Eng were the original "Siamese twins." Born in Siam (now Thailand) joined together, they may prove that reincarnation does not exist, according to some skeptics.

The Case of Corliss Chotkin Jr.

This case occurred in southeastern Alaska. Victor Vincent, a full-blooded Tlingit Indian, lived on an island off Alaska's southern coast. Near the end

72

of his life, he became close to his niece, Mrs. Corliss Chotkin, his sister's daughter.

Victor died in the spring of 1946. About a year before his death he predicted he would reincarnate as the Chotkin's next son. According to Stevenson, Victor told her, ''I hope I don't stutter then as much as I do now. Your son will have these scars.'' Victor then showed Mrs. Chotkin a scar on his back. It was from a back operation. He also pointed out a scar on the base of his nose on the right side. Victor claimed these scars would identify him as her next son.

On December 15, 1947, Mrs. Chotkin gave birth to a boy who was named after his father, Corliss Chotkin. The baby had two marks in the same shape and in the same location as Victor's!

Corliss's back scar was the more important to Stevenson. He thought it was characteristic of an operation scar. ''It was located about eight inches below the shoulder line and two inches to the right of midline. It was heavily pigmented, and, raised along its margins, one could still easily discern several small

Can scars and moles like these be used as evidence of reincarnation? Some proponents say they can, if the marks match those of a deceased person.

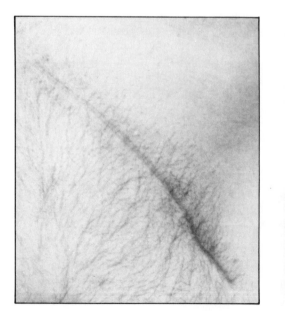

round marks outside the scar. Four of these on one side lined up like the stitch wounds of surgical operations.''

Not only did Corliss have birthmark scars, he also demonstrated behavioral characteristics similar to Victor's. Corliss was born with a stutter severe enough that he required special therapy for it when he was ten. Moreover, according to Stevenson, Corliss could handle boats well and repair their engines. He had no training. Victor had lived on boats.

Was Corliss the reincarnation of Victor?

How do we account for the marks—genetics? Stevenson says that heredity does not explain the birthmarks, for three reasons. One, the elongated mark on Corliss's back was heavily pigmented and not just an ordinary mole. The additional small marks around it suggested stitch marks. Two, Corliss was not a direct descendant of Victor Vincent. Three, Victor's scars were acquired from operations, not inherited, and this could not have been passed on genetically.

Stevenson believes Corliss's marks could have only one of two origins. They could have come from some accident in his mother's womb or from some other influence before conception. But Stevenson does

Corliss Chotkin Jr. had a birthmark very similar to the scar on the back of Victor Vincent.

not believe there was any accident—the birthmarks on the back too closely resembled a surgical wound.

Stevenson thinks the second alternative is better. Somehow the mind of Victor Vincent imprinted the scars on the baby in the womb—Corliss, who was really Victor.

How strong are birthmark cases as evidence of reincarnation? D. Scott Rogo believes such cases are weak. "Most of [Stevenson's] examples . . . highlight cases in which the child was allegedly reborn within his own family." Hence, they may have resulted from genetics.

Furthermore, Rogo states, the sampling is too small. If birthmark cases came from many different cultures, they might be stronger evidence. "We simply do not know how widespread these birthmark cases are."

This does not mean they can be easily dismissed, however. Rogo writes, "There is still the problem of just *how* these bizarre marks are formed in the first place. They certainly seem to go beyond anything modern genetics or biology can explain."

What do Stevenson's critics have to say about his cases? Stevenson describes the most frequent criticisms aimed at him:

The cases most occur where people already believe in reincarnation. If a child seems to refer to a previous life, it's argued that his parents encourage him and may unwittingly feed the child information about a deceased person. . . .

While this is a valid argument for a small number of cases, especially those occurring in the same family or village, it's inapplicable for long-distance cases where the child shows a detailed knowledge about a family his parents have never heard of, let alone met.

Stevenson's most severe critic is Ian Wilson, author of *All in the Mind*. Wilson asks, "Has he found something truly new and scientific or has he been cruelly misled by a series of tall stories and acting performances?"

In general, Wilson criticized Stevenson on several points. First, Stevenson has not found any rules governing reincarnation. For example, Wilson wonders, what determines the length of time between incarnations? What determines whether or not we shift nationality or location from one life to the next? What determines whether we are born within the same family or to an outside family?

Second, Wilson says Stevenson's cases come, for the most part, from cultures that traditionally believe in reincarnation. Might that not influence reincarnation claims?

Third, Wilson attacks the economic and social backgrounds of Stevenson's Indian and Sri Lankan cases. At least twenty out of the thirty past-life claims were that the individual in the previous life was wealthy or high class. Wilson writes, "From this information the possibility can scarcely be ignored that poor families may have tried to pass off their children as reincarnations of dead offspring of the rich in order to reap some financial advantage."

The beliefs in different cultures seem to affect the evidence about reincarnation. Does this mean that reincarnation takes place differently in different cultures? Or that people interpret the evidence to fit the ideas they already have? Or that reincarnation is simply a fantasy created in different cultures?

Fourth, Wilson argues that Stevenson has not provided photographs to support his birthmark cases.

D. Scott Rogo questions some of Wilson's arguments and feels that they are "hopelessly naive." One argument Rogo finds suspect is Wilson's observation about rules governing reincarnation. Rogo believes the rules and the process of reincarnation might be very complex, too complex to have been discovered yet.

Rogo also says that the charge about past-life cases involving the wealthy is true only of the Sri Lankan and Indian cases, not the Alaskan or Middle Eastern ones.

In regard to a lack of photographs, Stevenson has stated in his *Omni* magazine interview that, in the future, his books on reincarnation will contain photographs from cases in Burma, Turkey, Lebanon, and North America. Moreover, some cases will provide autopsy and medical records for birthmarks. "Such records provide the strongest evidence we have so far in favor of reincarnation," says Stevenson.

Cultural Influences

Are reincarnation claims fantasies based on local traditions and folklore? Do "laws" of reincarnation vary from culture to culture?

Based on Stevenson's research, Rogo outlines some data on cultural differences that have been found in reincarnation studies:

First, in Turkey, it is a local belief that only people who die violently will be reincarnated or remember past lives. This feature does not occur in Alaskan or Sri Lankan cases.

Second, rebirth cases in which the individual changes sex will usually occur only where the culture believes this is possible.

Third, reports of rebirths within the same family are common among the Tlingits, but rare in Turkey. Rogo says this "may reflect the fact that Tlingits are very concerned with family prestige."

Can a pregnant woman's dreams give clues about the past-life identity of her baby?

Fourth, apparent time periods between death and rebirth often correspond to the cultural and religious beliefs of an area. There are more reports of a person being reincarnated into a younger brother or sister or a direct descendant in the cultures that believe this happens.

Fifth, birthmark cases are common among Tlingits and in Turkey. This could reflect a Turkish belief that violent death leads to rebirth, while the Tlingits "emphasize the reappearance of such birthmarks."

Sixth, the dreams of pregnant mothers about a past-life identity becoming their offspring are common among Tlingits and in Turkey. They are rare in other Asian countries.

Could reincarnation claims merely fulfill cultural attitudes—people believe a certain way about reincarnation, hence they think it actually occurs? Stevenson argues that a person seeking rebirth may plan and execute it to conform to his or her cultural beliefs.

If hypnosis, spontaneous recall, special skills, and birthmarks don't absolutely prove the reincarnation issue, what does? Some say the answer lies in dreams and visions.

Five

Can We Get Clues About Reincarnation from Intuition?

Many people report experiences that hint at reincarnation. Some of them appear more as intuitive flashes than actual memory. In other words, these intuitive experiences seem to come from deeper levels of the mind than memory. Such experiences, too, are briefer and more intense than memory.

The most common of these are dreams, visions, and déjà vu. One girl, for example, dreamt of being executed in London in a past life:

The dream was of being a prisoner in a place that I knew to be the Tower of London. I had not seen it in real life, but I had no doubt where I was. It was very cold weather. . . . I was aware that I had been condemned to death. This, I used to dream over and over again, and after being in the dream a vigorous man, to wake up and be a little girl felt rather strange.

At last the dream changed, and I was standing on a scaffold which must have been newly erected as it smelt of sawdust. Everything was decorous and decent. The executioner knelt and apologised for what

Opposite: A young girl dreamed of being a prisoner in the Tower of London. Was this evidence of reincarnation or simply a fantasy?

he was about to do. I took the axe from his hand and felt it, and handed it back, bidding him to do his duty.

Was the young girl's dream suggestive of reincarnation?

Visions

Dr. Fredrick Lenz is a San Diego-based psychologist and author of *Lifetimes, True Accounts of Reincarnation*. He has collected more than 120 accounts of reincarnation, some of them emerging in visions. Consider this account given by one of Lenz's subjects, a physician from Connecticut.

One day in late October I was outside in my yard raking leaves. I had been working hard all morning, and I felt it was time for a break. I sat down under a maple tree and was starting to relax when my whole body began to shake violently. I lost awareness of where I was, and all I could see was blackness in all directions. I felt I was plunging down a long black tunnel; I was nauseated from the falling. Then I began to see light at the end of the tunnel. I found myself sitting upright in a chair in my living room. One of

One of Fredrick Lenz's subjects "dreamed" of falling through a tunnel into another time and place.

my servants approached me and told me that my horse was ready for my trip into town. I followed him outside the house, mounted my horse, and rode into town. I remember that I passed a group of merchants on camels on the way to town. They were all acquaintances of mine, and each one paused for a moment of brief conversation. We discussed the weather and the state of the crops. After each encounter, I continued my journey toward town. Arriving in town, I dismounted and entered a drinking house. There I joined several of my friends and we drank and joked for some time. The thing that stands out in my mind the most was how real everything was. I could see the crowds of people inside, feel the metal goblet in my hands, taste the drink. . . .

A fight broke out, and there was yelling and cursing. I was thrown violently to the floor. Before I could raise myself up I was kicked in the head and I lost consciousness. I found myself surrounded by blackness again. . . . I found I had returned to the present. I was sitting up straight under the maple tree in my backyard.

Was this vision based on an actual past life? How can we tell? Are there any patterns in such visions that point to reincarnation?

In the above account, the subject describes certain sensations at the beginning of his experience. Most of Lenz's subjects report similar sensations, which D. Scott Rogo in *The Search for Yesterday* has termed the "Lenz syndrome." Lenz says his subjects go through a series of stages in their intuitive experiences before connecting with memories of a past life. The stages leading to actual visions are as mysterious as the reincarnation visions themselves.

He lists these stages of sensations:

(a) Sound. Subjects reported hearing a "high-pitched ringing" in the first stage. The sound would overpower all other sound.

As an example, Lenz provides an account by one subject, Harry, who, in his vision, saw a former life

"Everything in the mind comes from what has gone on before."

Dr. Norris Netherton, psychiatrist

"It is . . . difficult to believe that memories could persist after the destruction of the physical brain."

Scientist Douglas M. Stokes

A woman's astral body floats outside her physical one.

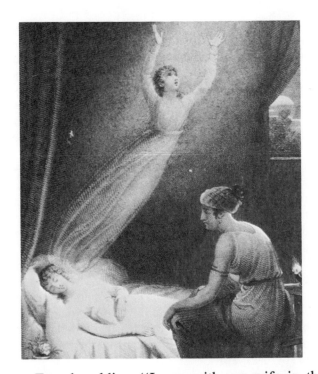

as a French soldier. "I was with my wife in the bedroom. It had been a normal day. The kids were in bed and I had just put on my bathrobe. I began to hear a ringing sound. I almost didn't notice it at first, but it kept getting louder and louder. I asked my wife if she knew where the sound was coming from. She told me she didn't hear anything. I told her I had a loud ringing sound in my ears. She told me to go to bed and forget it and that it would be gone in the morning. I was very upset. I went downstairs to the living room and turned on the TV. I thought that if I watched for a couple of minutes it might go away. The sound didn't leave me, though; it kept getting louder. It finally got so loud that I couldn't even hear the TV."

(b) Feeling of weightlessness. Lenz's subjects report they felt as if they were floating during their experiences. One subject, Leonard, said, "My body was numb and weightless."

According to Fredrick Lenz, many people, like this man, experience great joy when they make a connection with a past life.

(c) Color. Lenz says the majority of his subjects "saw flashes of brilliant color at the onset of their remembrance." One reported: "I kept seeing these bright bursts of color. They were mostly in the blue and gold range. I watched the colors move and shimmer. How could I describe it except to say they were the most beautiful colors I have ever seen."

(d) Vibrations. Lenz's subjects reported that everything around them began to vibrate. The vibrations could be seen, felt, and heard. Lenz states the subjects "believed that these vibrations unlocked an inner door that led to the memories of their past lives."

(e) Feeling of well-being. Lenz's subjects reported feelings of peace and joy during their experiences. They were not terrified. One subject, Pamela, told Lenz, "I never wanted it to stop. All I could see was light, an ocean of light."

(f) Knowing without thinking. Some subjects reported they had access to all knowledge. Answers

People who "experience" a past life say it often feels like watching a movie.

would come to them about questions before they had even formed the question. One subject reported, "I knew more about life in those few minutes than from all the perceptions and ideas that I had formulated during an entire lifetime."

(g) The movie. According to Lenz, the subjects would see images and scenes in their minds, as if they were watching a movie. Lenz writes, "They feel as if they are viewing portions of their past history the way a scientist would observe a specimen under a microscope." One subject reported, "The impression I had was that I was being shown scenes from my past life for my own educational benefit. At times it was like seeing a movie in which I was the star."

(h) Full participation. In this stage, Lenz explains, most people described actually experiencing, or participating in, the vision, not just watching it.

Are these visions real scenes from past lives? Why do they occur in stages? Why do they happen to some people but not to others?

Time Frames

D. Scott Rogo, in *The Search for Yesterday*, suggests that some visions may be what one of Rogo's subjects called "switching time frames." Rogo did his own study on visionary experiences. He found his subjects were "suddenly transported in time and momentarily *living* a scene from a past life." In other words, subjects had visions of a strange place while they were aware and active.

According to Rogo, such experiences may be retro-cognitive (perceiving the past); a subject mentally tunes into a past time and place. They may become so caught up in the sights and sounds of a past time that they confuse everyday reality with the scene.

He cites one woman's brief account of switching time frames. She was riding in a golf cart on a golf course with her husband. "We were going down a very rough path through the trees, very fast, when for a few seconds I felt like I had switched time frames. We were in England, clattering down a country path in a cart drawn by a horse."

What explains this? Rogo believes the best explanation is that such visions result from spontaneous

This woman, riding a golf cart, suddenly felt herself in the past riding a farmer's horse-drawn wagon.

"The dreams of our present life are the environment in which we work out the impressions, thoughts, feelings, of a former life."

Leo Tolstoy, Russian novelist

"To believe literally in reincarnation may be the result of a confusion. Using the analogy of the dream, it means that you confuse your *subjective*, conscious self with the changing *content* or object of a series of dreams or with a sequence within one dream."

Author Peter Koestenbaum, *Is There an Answer to Death?*

electrical activity in the brain. Hence, they could be mistaken for reincarnation visions. A person may have a tiny electrical seizure in the brain which results in feeling or seeing a past life.

However, Rogo suggests it is possible that the emergence of deeply buried memories may actually trigger neural (nerve) firings! Neural firings may not be the cause of past-life experiences but the result.

Altered States

Rogo believes the Lenz syndrome occurs when a person enters an altered state of consciousness. Rogo defines an altered state of consciousness as a mental state that differs from our day-to-day awareness. In our everyday kind of awareness, we perceive grass as being green. In an altered sense of awareness, we might perceive grass as being blue.

These altered states share certain features with Lenz's syndrome, where the attention of the mind is directed inward rather than outward. In our daily awareness, we perceive objects outside of ourselves. When our perception is directed inward, we perceive objects in our minds, as in a daydream, for example.

Rogo notes that if past-life memories exist deep within the brain's storage bank, then we must enter a state of mind where these memories can be tapped. Rogo thinks an altered state of consciousness, resulting in a vision, may serve to open up these memory banks.

Rogo observes an interesting aspect of Lenz's cases. Most of Lenz's subjects had no prior "interest or belief in reincarnation," although their experiences promoted a "strong conviction" toward reincarnation afterwards.

Dreams

Unlike altered states of consciousness, dreaming is a common experience. Lenz provides an account of a past-life dream from his subject, Pamela Cohen, a hospital worker in Canada.

I saw my past life in Kentucky in a dream I had

Pamela Cohen, a Canadian, remembered a past life in the Old South.

several years ago. I saw that I was in the Old South. The roads were all muddy, and I had to pick up my skirts to walk across the street. As I was walking across the street, I could hear the noises of the wheels on the wagons turning, smell the horses, feel the heat of the day. I started off the dream looking at my feet in the mud, and I picked up my blue skirts, and walked across the street to the stairs for the sidewalk. Instead of having steps that went straight up, you had to enter them from the side. Then I walked into the general store, and as I walked in I was totally at home. It was like breathing a breath of relief. There were other people in the store, but they didn't mean anything to me. I had the feeling that my life was very hard and drab. Coming to the general store was very exciting. I bought some red thread and calico material for a dress. I almost bought a blue ribbon for my hair, but I knew that I shouldn't spend that money.

I knew this was not an ordinary dream. While I was experiencing all of this, there was such an intense feeling of familiarity about it all. It was like, ''Oh, I'm home again! I haven't seen this place for so long! I know this place!''

Did Pamela actually dream of a past life? Perhaps. The dream was unusual in its familiarity and its detail.

Occasionally a past-life experience will be violent and unpleasant.

In general, Lenz has noted four ways that past-life dreams differ from regular ones. These are:

(1) The [past-life] dream remembrance was accompanied by sensations completely unlike those they have experienced in any other dreams; (2) during the dream remembrance, [the dreamers] were aware that they were seeing one or more of their past lives; (3) unlike most dreams, which normally fade after several hours or months, dream remembrances are so vivid the dreamer can describe even the slightest details of [the] dream years later; and (4) after someone has had a remembrance dream, he [or she] changes . . . attitudes toward death and dying.

In Pamela's case, she asserts she was conscious that her dream was of a past life. Moreover, her dream fits most of the ways Lenz points out that a past-life dream differs from a regular one.

Do such dreams prove reincarnation? D. Scott Rogo in *The Search for Yesterday* says, "Not really." But what impresses Rogo is a pattern that emerged from his own research into reincarnation dreams.

The dreams he documented were "all violent and usually relate to the dreamer's death." Rogo believes if reincarnation is a fact, then this pattern is just the type of experience that would emerge. "One's death, especially if it occurred violently or tragically, might be expected to impress itself forcefully on the new life."

Rogo notes that Stevenson, too, found a similar pattern in children's past lives. But as Rogo points out, skeptics might argue that death-reincarnation dreams result from some obscure psychological reason. For example, perhaps a person has a desire to die and fulfills that wish through dreams. Or maybe the dream of a past life merely reflects a person's desire to survive physical death.

Rogo, however, finds that death is not a prominent theme in normal dreaming, and reincarnation best explains these dream cases.

Déjà Vu

Have you ever experienced a feeling of having been some place before? If so, you may have had a déjà vu experience. Déjà vu means "already seen."

Rogo reports a déjà vu account of one of his subjects:

Actress Shirley MacLaine claims to have lived several past lives. She has written several best-selling books that include details of some of her incarnations.

> We were driving down the New Jersey Turnpike, and I felt very strange, all this landscape was very familiar to me. . . . I turned to Joanne, and said, "You know, I have never been here before, but I believe about a mile or so down the road is a house I used to live in."
>
> As we went down the turnpike, (heading north), everything was familiar . . . the older houses, and I began describing *what* we would see before we came to it.
>
> Approximately three miles or so passed, and I told my friend that around the bend, we would come to a small town; it was set very close to the turnpike. I told her that the houses would be white frame, two-story homes, rather close together . . . and that I felt that I lived there when I was six years old or so, and that I used to sit with my "granny" on the front porch. The memories overwhelmed me, and I could

Driving through the countryside, one man suddenly "recognized" a place he had lived in a past life.

remember sitting on the swing, on the front porch, and my grandmother buttoning up my high-topped shoes. I could not do it myself. When we got to the town, I recognized the house immediately, only the front porch swing was not there. . . . However, at the time I lived there with my Granny, there was also wicker furniture on the porch with green cloth cushions. . . . I tried to get Joanne to let me direct her to the cemetery where ''I'' was buried, but she was so frightened that she would not take the drive. . . .

We got on the turnpike again, and went on to Paterson . . . and I still know that once, round the early 1900s, that I lived there, and died there.

Did Rogo's subject really live before?

C.J. Ducasse, author of *The Belief in a Life After Death*, believes déjà vu experiences reflect memories of a similar experience we have already had in our *present* life.

For example, perhaps you see a bridge you think you have seen in a past life. In fact, according to Ducasse's reasoning, you may have seen a similar bridge in this life and only now remember it.

D. Scott Rogo writes that déjà vu experiences could provide direct evidence for reincarnation. But do déjà vu experiences, along with dreams and visions, *prove* reincarnation?

Rogo says that ''no matter how suggestive these reports appear to be, they fall short of formal proof. Not enough information is contained in most of them that *can* be documented,'' such as names, dates, and places.

According to Rogo, however, the value of such cases is that they seem to follow certain patterns and cannot be fully explained. Reincarnation might be the explanation.

Six

What Happens Between Lives?

If we survive bodily death, and reincarnation is a fact, what happens between death and rebirth? Indeed, what exactly survives? A soul? A personality? Let us examine the possibilities.

Soul

In the West, our understanding of reincarnation has its roots in the Vedantic, or Hindu, philosophy from India.

Vedantism teaches that there is an ultimate reality, or God (Brahma), which creates *jivas*, the Christian equivalent of souls. According to Vedantism, once created, souls reincarnate until they reunite with God.

Reincarnation occurs for spiritual progression, says Vedantism. People progress to the point where they become aware they were never, in actuality, separate from God, just as a wave is never actually separated from the ocean.

What keeps people from this awareness? According to Vedantism, it is our perception of ourselves in the world. We perceive ourselves as separate from God and the world. Vedantism argues that no person

Opposite: A Tibetan version of the "Cycle of Transmigrations," the various states a person might go through before reaching the end of the cycle of life.

C.J. Ducasse believes that reincarnation is possible.

is an island. Everyone shares the same ocean. Until people realize this, they continue the cycle of death and rebirth.

Yet there is speculation whether souls actually exist. J. Paul Williams, in a *Yale Review* article, wrote: "The [best] argument for a future life . . . is the simple one that if man is a soul it is not unreasonable to suppose that he survives death. . . . The case for the future life is no stronger than is the case for the existence of the soul. Are human beings souls?"

An objection to the soul theory is that if we have souls and reincarnate, why don't we remember past lives?

As we have seen, some people do remember, but the majority of us do not. Yet the absence of memory may not disprove the soul and reincarnation. Says C.J. Ducasse, in his book *Nature, Mind, and Death*, "If the absence of memory of having existed at a certain

Mohandas Gandhi, one of the most influential men in the modern world, was a devout Hindu and believer in reincarnation.

time proved that we did not exist at that time, it would then prove far too much; for it would prove that we did not exist during the first few years of the life of our present body, nor on most of the days since then [since we don't remember our early years and even a lot of what has happened in more recent years]. . . . Lack of memory of lives earlier than our present one is therefore no evidence at all that we did not live before.''

If we have souls that reincarnate, perhaps it is best that we do not remember, suggested Mohandas K. Gandhi, social philosopher of India. In his *Letters to a Disciple*, published in 1950, he wrote, ''It is nature's kindness that we do not remember past births. Where is the good . . . of knowing in detail the numberless births we have gone through? Life would be a burden if we carried such a tremendous load of memories.''

C.J. Ducasse leads us to another possibility. He suggests that what might be reborn is not a soul, but some aspect or part of a previous personality. For example, a skill, habit, belief, or interest. Whether such an aspect will reemerge in a new body depends upon how strong it was in a previous life.

His idea is akin to Buddhism's way of looking at reincarnation.

Relative Elements

D. Scott Rogo, in *The Search for Yesterday*, states that in Buddhist thinking the concept of a soul is rejected. The mind, rather than the soul, is viewed as the ultimate ''seat of the self.'' The mind is real, yet temporary. Hence, to the Buddhist, there is no soul— just a temporary and changing mind.

Furthermore, Buddhists regard the mind as a stream of thought. For example, if you could record and see every thought your mind had in a twenty-four-hour period, your mind would probably appear as a stream of constantly moving and changing thoughts. One second you're thinking of a friend, the next you're

''Repeated instances have been reported . . . of body-soul separation for varied periods of time. The victim has been able to accurately recall and account for many minute details that occurred in the room after having been pronounced 'dead.'''

Scientist quoted by George Gallup Jr., *Adventures in Immortality*

''These [near-death experiences] are undoubtedly cerebral [brain] manifestations which the subjects recall. The individual has not died in the episode as is evident by his or her return to consciousness, and cerebral activity has *not* ceased (no 'brain death').''

Physician quoted by George Gallup Jr., *Adventures in Immortality*

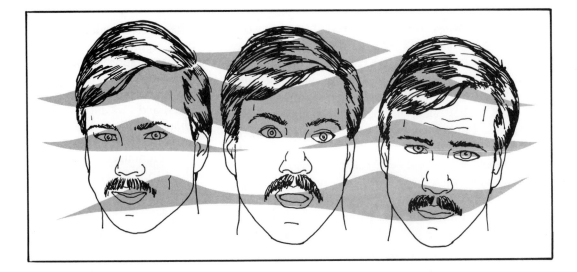

Buddhists view the mind as the ''seat of the self.'' It is constantly changing, never permanent.

thinking of a homework problem.

Hence, if you are your thoughts, then you have no permanent self. The kinds of things you think about now will not be the same in five years. According to Rogo's interpretation of Buddhism, we are a process of behaviors or elements that are changing constantly:

Buddhism doesn't even talk about reincarnation, only about rebirth. The concept of rebirth stems from the Buddhist idea that each of us is a temporary and changing configuration of elements consisting of our body, feelings, perceptions, moral will, and consciousness.

What survives after death, in the Buddhist view, ''is a constellation of character dispositions [personality traits].''

Rogo notes a common Buddhist metaphor for rebirth—one candle lighting another. ''The second candle does not become the first candle, but it somehow carries on its heritage.''

Psychon

The late British philosopher, Whately Carington, argues a position close to Buddhism's.

Carington believed the mind is a network of images and sensory data. He called it a "psychon" system. He held that the network was linked together by common ideas, which he called "K" ideas.

Rogo states the value of such a system—one system could integrate with another under certain conditions. "For example, two minds could link together (telepathically) if at a certain time they share a number of associated ideas."

In other words, Rogo explains, what survives death isn't a unique personality, but a network of ideas and experiences somewhat contaminated by the psychon systems "we have 'picked up' from other people." For example, a psychon system (the donor) may attach itself to a newborn child by infiltrating its newly developing personality. Or, Rogo writes, a newborn child or embryo might seek out and telepathically link with a free-floating psychon system with which it shares common idea patterns.

Whately Carington believed the mind is a network of images and sensory data called a psychon system. He believed one mind could "imprint" itself on another, thereby causing a kind of reincarnation, or rebirth, of at least part of a person's mind.

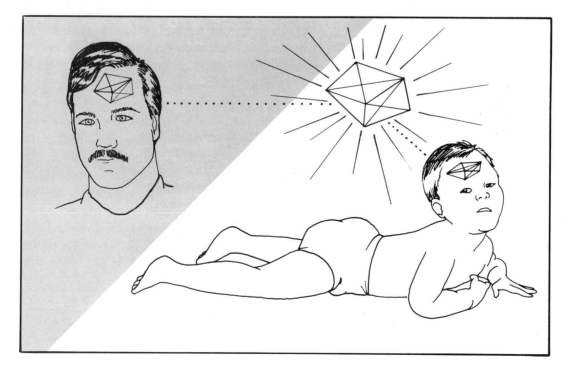

Psychologist Dr. Gardner Murphy suggested that a psychon system could be attracted to an embryo developing in its own culture and become attached to it because of their mutual cultural backgrounds. When a child remembers a past life, it might be recalling the memories of a dead personality.

Rogo expresses an interesting point, though. He says each psychon system would probably weaken in time and dissolve. Consequently, this might explain why children have past-life memories that fade away after they reach about six years of age.

John H. Hick, a theologian at Claremont College in California, theorizes that "after bodily death a mental 'husk' or 'mask' of the deceased person is left behind and is telepathically accessible (retrieved by ESP) under certain conditions to living persons."

Hick also says, "There is no rebirth of the full living personality. But there is a kind of reincarnation of parts or aspects of the personality."

Could it be that we are a mixture of other people's personalities? Or do we have individual souls? When we die, what happens between death and reincarnation? Do we sleep and dream? Are we awake? Ancient Tibetans may have the answer.

Tibetan Book of the Dead

The *Bardo Thodol*, or *The Tibetan Book of the Dead*, written in about the eighth century, was read to dying persons during their last moments and during funeral ceremonies. It served two functions. It aided the dying person in recognizing the nature of the experience as he or she died. It also reminded the living to think positively for the deceased. This would help the deceased to release his or her earthly bonds with family and physical life. It would help reduce the deceased person's confusion in the death state.

The book is a spiritual guide to the after-death state. It describes various states, or *Bardos*, a deceased person might experience. After death, the book says,

the deceased finds himself or herself on a plane of consciousness between lives. There are three initial stages:

- *Chikkai Bardo*. According to *The Tibetan Book of the Dead*, people may find themselves in a dark void. They may hear sounds described as roaring, thundering, and whistling. They may then encounter a blissful, clear light, the radiance of their true nature. Along with its presence, people may experience serenity and joy. If people's consciousness is as pure as the light, they may merge with the light. If not, their consciousness will fall away from it.

- *Chónyid Bardo*. In this bardo, people may find themselves outside of the body and looking at it, or they may witness family members and try, in vain, to contact them. Also in this bardo, people may have visions of peaceful or frightening beings. According to a person's karma, if the person has led a good life, the visions will be heavenly; if a bad life, they will be hellish. These things are, in actuality, aspects of one's own self.

- *Sidpa Bardo*. After the Chónyid Bardo, people may find themselves reviewing their entire past lives as if in a mirror, scrutinizing every deed. They then judge the deeds and begin preparing for the next life. People's station in the next life will be determined by

An artist's drawing of a small segment from the *Tibetan Book of the Dead*.

This drawing, from William Blake's book *The Grave* (1808), shows one conception of a person's essence, or soul, floating outside the body. In this case, it shows a Christian view. The soul is not reborn into a different body; it travels to an afterlife in heaven, purgatory, or hell.

their deeds in the past.

Duration

How long after death before we reincarnate? It seems there is no fixed stay.

Joe Fisher, in his book *The Case for Reincarnation*, writes, "Reports range from whistlestops of several hours to extended settlements of hundreds of years."

In Jane Roberts's book, *The Nature of Personal Reality*, her spiritual guide, Seth, responded to the question of what determines the duration between lives: "You. If you are very tired, then you rest. If you are wise, you take time to digest your knowledge and plan your next life, even as a writer plans his next book. If you have too many ties with this reality or if you are impatient, or if you have not learned sufficiently, then you may return too quickly. It is always up to the individual. There is no predestination [fixed destiny]. The answers are within yourself then, as the answers are within you now."

Dr. Ian Stevenson also addresses the question of time between lives. In an article in the *Journal of the*

Some people believe that human beings can only be reincarnated from other people; others believe we can experience the lives of animals as well.

American Society for Psychical Research in October 1974, he suggests that the modern world is more speeded up than in past centuries. Consequently, the intermission between lives could now be much shorter than previously. Plato, in his dialogue *Republic*, mentions a thousand-year cycle of rebirth.

Population

Moreover, Stevenson estimates that each human has lived an average of twenty incarnations. Why? Because the world's present population is about 5 billion. Researchers estimate a total of between 69 billion and 96 billion people have lived on earth, averaging 80 billion. Divide 80 billion by the present population, 5 billion, and each of us may have lived twenty times.

This brings up another question. If everyone is reincarnated, why does the world's population keep growing. Is there a set number of people who can reincarnate, or are new souls continually being created?

Stevenson suggests that conceivably human souls evolve and graduate to human bodies from those of

Many people who have lived through a near-death experience report floating through a tunnel.

animals. Is this possible? Would the mass extinctions of animals in recent times account for the human population explosion?

Furthermore, Stevenson doesn't dismiss the possibility that human souls may have "emigrated from other solar systems to ours."

Near-Death Research

Some near-death researchers have found striking parallels between near-death descriptions and those in *The Tibetan Book of the Dead*. These descriptions are remarkably similar to the experiences some people have had during their visions of past lives (the Lenz syndrome). New or ancient, these descriptions indicate we may indeed survive death. If we survive death, perhaps we also reincarnate.

What is a near-death experience? It is an experience some people claim to have while they have been believed to be dead either from an accident or an illness.

According to Dr. Raymond A. Moody, author of *Life After Life*, what people report is fantastic. They report being outside of their bodies, seeing a bright light, being in a tunnel or void, hearing ringing and buzzing noises, feeling peaceful and free, having clear perceptions, being surprised at still being alive, and losing their fear of death.

Individuals may have one or several of these experiences. Moody gives an example of what typically happens:

> A man is dying and, as he reaches the point of greatest physical distress, he hears himself pronounced dead by his doctor. He begins to hear an uncomfortable noise, a loud ringing or buzzing, and at the same time feels himself moving very rapidly through a long dark tunnel. After this, he suddenly finds himself outside his own physical body, but still in the immediate physical environment, and he sees his own body from a distance, as though he is a spectator. He watches the resuscitation attempt from this

A near-death experience: The subject feels as though she is outside her own body. Do such experiences provide possible evidence in favor of reincarnation?

unusual vantage point and is in a state of emotional upheaval.

Soon other things begin to happen. Others come to meet and to help him. He glimpses the spirits of relatives and friends who have already died, and a loving, warm spirit of a kind he has never encountered before—a being of light—appears before him. This being asks him a question, nonverbally, to make him evaluate his life and helps him along by showing him a panoramic, instantaneous playback of the major events of his life. . . . He is overwhelmed by intense feelings of joy, love, and peace. Despite his attitude, though, he somehow reunites with his physical body and lives.

Moody explains that the order of experiences a person goes through varies with each individual. And not all dying persons have such experiences. Some reported having none of them.

These experiences do suggest, though, there might be life after death. Why are some aspects of near-death descriptions so similar to what people experienced during past-life visions, as Dr. Lenz found in his studies?

Moody is intrigued and fascinated by near-death reports, but draws no conclusions. Do we live after death? If evidence suggests that we do, will we reincarnate?

Epilogue

The Search Goes On

Has the mystery of reincarnation been solved? Hardly. But researchers will continue to explore the phenomenon, and people will continue to have memories, visions, and dreams of past lives.

Ian Wilson, in his book *All in the Mind*, writes: "We are each of us passengers in the exploration of a vast universe within ourselves, a dynamic, ever-restless kaleidoscope of images, ideas, dreams, emotions, and more, the complexity and extent of which we have scarcely yet begun to grasp."

Perhaps the truth of the mystery of reincarnation waits inside of us, until we ourselves cross the threshold between life and death.

In his poem "East Coker," T.S. Eliot wrote, "In my beginning is my end. . . .In my end is my beginning." Do people really live a myriad of lives, or do they have only one life to live as best they can?

Bibliography

Linda Atkinson, *Have We Lived Before?* New York: Dodd, Mead & Company, 1981.

Morey Bernstein, *The Search for Bridey Murphy.* Garden City, NY: Doubleday & Company, 1956.

David Christie-Murray, *Reincarnation: Ancient Beliefs and Modern Evidence.* London: Newton Abbot, 1981.

Sylvia Cranston & Carey Williams, *Reincarnation: A New Horizon in Science, Religion, and Society.* New York: Julian Press, 1984.

S.L. Cranston & Joseph Head, eds., *Reincarnation in World Thought.* New York: Julian Press, 1967.

C.J. Ducasse, *The Belief in a Life After Death.* Springfield, IL: Charles C. Thomas Publishers, 1961.

C.J. Ducasse, *Nature, Mind, and Death.* LaSalle, IL: Open Court, 1951.

Joe Fisher, *The Case for Reincarnation.* New York: Bantam Books, 1985.

Hans Holzer, *Born Again.* Garden City, NY: Doubleday & Company, 1970.

Geddes MacGregor, ed., *Immortality and Human Destiny.* New York: Paragon House, 1985.

Raymond A. Moody, *Life After Life.* Boston: G.K. Hall & Co., 1977.

D. Scott Rogo, *The Search for Yesterday.* Englewood Cliffs, NJ: Prentice-Hall, Inc., 1985.

Ian Stevenson, *Twenty Cases of the Reincarnation Type.* Charlottesville, VA: University Press of Virginia, 1975.

Ian Stevenson, *Twenty Cases Suggestive of Reincarnation.* Charlottesville, VA: University Press of Virginia, 1966.

Helen Wambach, *Reliving Past Lives.* New York: Harper & Row, 1978.

Ian Wilson, *The After Death Experience.* New York: William Morrow & Company, 1987.

Ian Wilson, *All in the Mind.* Garden City, NY: Doubleday & Company, 1982.

Index

Picture Credits

About the Author

Michael Arvey is a freelance writer who has lived all over the U.S. He currently works as an editor and teaches correspondence courses in creative writing. At various times, he has also been a meditation instructor, massage therapist, and poet.